BARRON'S

A Pocket Guide to
Synonyms

Arthur H. Bell, Ph.D.
Georgetown University
Washington, D.C.

BARRON'S EDUCATIONAL SERIES, INC.

All inquiries should be addressed to:
Barron's Educational Series, Inc.
250 Wireless Boulevard
Hauppauge, New York 11788

Library of Congress Catalog Card No.: 91-38291

International Standard Book No. 0-8120-4843-1

Library of Congress Cataloging-in-Publication Data

Bell, Arthur H. (Arthur Henry), 1946–
    A pocket guide to synonyms : highlighting the most overused
words in college and business / by Arthur H. Bell.
        p.   cm.
    ISBN (invalid) 0-8120-4843-0
    1. English language—Synonyms and antonyms.   I. Title.
PE1591.B426 1992
423'.1—dc20   91-38291
                                                                  CIP

PRINTED IN THE UNITED STATES OF AMERICA
2345   5500   987654321

Introduction

When was the last time you needed just the right word? Like most writers, you probably search for synonyms in almost every paragraph you compose. Let's say, for example, you have used the word *brave* in the first sentence of a paragraph. You want to refer to bravery in later sentences as well—but repeating the word *brave* sounds awkward and repetitious. In fact, most writers know the frustration of trying to find what Jonathan Swift called, "the right word for the right place."

Synonyms to the rescue! By using this alphabetical guide, you can quickly glance at many possible substitutes for *brave*, including *fearless, heroic, brave-hearted, steadfast, courageous,* and *valiant.* Thanks to a handy menu of such synonym choices at your side, you can write more quickly and more gracefully.

Just as important, you may express yourself more accurately and fully. Looking over a list of synonyms gives you the chance to pick the precise word that captures your intended meaning.

Gathered in the *Pocket Guide to Synonyms* are more than 20,000 root words and synonyms. They have been selected for their usefulness in writing tasks for your academic and career life. A special list, The Most Overused Words in School and Career Writing, is provided and these words are also marked with a • within the *Guide.* Using these words requires particular care. All of the marked words are very familiar—but that is just the problem. In many cases, they have become threadbare from repeated use. Therefore, the • highlight in the *Guide* is the signal that you are looking at an overused word. A synonym may often be advisable in its place. To help you on your way, a full-sentence example using such a synonym has been provided for each of the marked words in the *Guide.*

In some cases, a word may have distinctly different meanings and, therefore, different sets of synonyms. The word *minute*, for example, can mean a unit of time or *minuscule* (as in "a minute amount"). Throughout the *Guide*, a semicolon (;) is used to separate these different sets of synonyms.

Standard dictionary abbreviations are used to identify parts of speech: N., noun; V., verb; ADJ., adjective; ADV., adverb. Occasionally, the synonyms for an entry word will function as two parts of speech. These may be indicated as N., V. followed by the synonyms.

The Most Overused Words in School and Career Writing

Because they are both useful and common, the following words are often overused. This *Guide* provides full-sentence examples showing synonym alternatives for these overused words, identified by a •.

additionally	begin	comprehend
adequate	behavior	comput
adjust	believe	conceive
adopt	belong	concept
advisable	beneficial	concern
agreement	besides	condition
alienate	bizarre	confuse
all right	blame	connect
almost	bore	conscious
also	brief	consequence
amazing	brilliant	consider
analyze	build	considerable
apparent	bunch	consideration
appearance	business	consistent
approximately	busy	control
argument	capable	convenient
ascertain	capacity	cooperate
assertion	careful	creative
assess	casual	crisis
assistance	cause	crucial
assume	certainly	decide
attention	challenge	decrease
attitude	change	definite
authorize	claim	deliver
available	clarify	demand
avoid	combination	depend
awful	common	describe
barely	communicate	determine
basically	company	develop
beautiful	compete	difference

direct	guess	manage
discover	happy	mankind
discuss	help	matter
distribute	helpful	maybe
duty	helpless	meaning
easy	hesitate	meaningful
economical	hinder	mental
educate	honest	minimum
efficiency	honesty	misconception
eliminate	hope	mistake
emphasize	hopeful	money
employ	hostile	mostly
enable	huge	motivate
enlighten	idea	natural
environment	ignorant	nature
equal	imagination	necessary
essential	immediate	necessity
establish	immense	nice
evident	importance	nonsense
example	important	nothing
excellent	impossible	objection
exceptional	impression	obvious
expectation	improve	occur
explain	inadequate	opportunity
explore	increase	option
express	indicate	ordinary
extreme	individual	organize
fact	inefficient	original
factor	influence	outstanding
false	influential	participate
famous	initial	people
favorite	insecure	personal
feel	insist	physical
flexible	interest	place
follow	interpretation	pleasing
frequent	involve	point
fulfill	irrelevant	point of view
function	issue	popular
fundamental	justify	position
future	know	possess
general	limit	possible
generate	logic	practical
good	luck	precisely

pretend
previous
primary
probable
project
provide
purpose
qualify
quality
question
ready
reality
really
receive
recognize
regular
relative
remarkable
review
satisfactory

schedule
sensitive
several
significance
situation
society
solution
specific
standard
strengthen
substantial
suggestion
superior
suppose
technique
temporary
tendency
tension
terrific
thorough

tremendous
trivial
typical
unconscious
undeniable
understand
undesirable
unfavorable
unlimited
unnecessary
unreasonable
usually
vague
valuable
variety
weak
weird
worthless
young

A

abandon V. desert, quit, forsake, leave.

abate V. decrease, diminish, reduce, subside.

abbreviate V. shorten, reduce, condense, contract.

abdicate V. forsake, renounce, relinquish, give up.

abdication N. renunciation, abandonment, resignation.

abduct V. kidnap, seize, shanghai, capture, steal.

aberrance N. abnormality, deviation.

aberrant ADJ. abnormal, errant.

aberration N. deviation, irregularity, insanity, abnormality.

abeyance N. latency, inaction, suspension, reservation.

abhor V. despise, hate, loathe, dislike, detest.

abhorrence N. hate, horror.

abide V. dwell, reside, live, remain.

ability N. capability, skill, ableness, faculty.

abjure V. retract, take back, repudiate.

ablaze ADJ. blazing, fiery, burning.

able ADJ. competent, proficient, capable, qualified.

able-bodied ADJ. strapping, sturdy, strong.

abnormal ADJ. uncommon, peculiar, odd, unnatural, irregular.

abnormality N. aberrance, anomalism, deviation.

abode N. home, dwelling, residence.

abolish V. erase, obliterate, undo, revoke, negate.

abolition N. negation, annulment, nullification.

abominable ADJ. horrible, loathsome, disgusting, hateful, unspeakable.

aboriginal ADJ. native, prehistoric, primeval.

abort V. miscarry, stop, terminate, kill, sever.

abound V. flourish, overflow, teem.

about ADV. nearly, approximately;—PREP. relating to, concerning, involving, having to do with.

abridge V. condense, shorten, abbreviate, cut.

abrogate V. cancel, revoke, abolish, annul, nullify.

abrupt ADJ. sudden, short, brusque, hurried, blunt.

abscond V. flee, retreat, escape, disappear, steal away.

absence N. want, need, lack, defect.

absent ADJ. missing, void, away, lacking.

absentminded ADJ. inattentive, forgetful, preoccupied.

absolute ADJ. complete, thorough, perfect, total, entire, unlimited.

absolutely ADV. positively, doubtlessly, definitely.

absolve V. pardon, forgive, exonerate, acquit.

absorb V. consume, engross, incorporate, digest.

absorbed ADJ. engrossed, consumed, preoccupied, rapt.

absorbent ADJ. absorptive, assimilating, bibulous.

absorbing ADJ. gripping, enthralling, engrossing.

absorption N. engrossment, preoccupation, assimilation.

abstain V. refrain, fast, forbear.

abstemious ADJ. temperate, abstinent.

abstinence N. continence, temperance, abstention, self-denial, fasting.

abstract ADJ. theoretical;—N. synopsis;—V. remove, detach, separate.

abstracted ADJ. engrossed, absentminded, withdrawn, oblivious, preoccupied.

abstruse ADJ. profound, difficult, abstract.

absurd ADJ. foolish, ridiculous, senseless.

absurdity N. foolishness, insanity, ridiculousness.

abundance N. opulence, plenty.

abundant ADJ. plentiful, opulent, lavish, profuse.

abuse V. scorn, disgrace, defame, injure, violate, malign.

abusive ADJ. damaging, slanderous, invective.

abysmal ADJ. terrible, horrible, awful, deep, yawning.

academic ADJ. scholastic, scholarly, learned, literary.

accede V. concur, agree, consent, assent.

accelerate V. hasten, quicken, facilitate, expedite, hurry.

accent N. tone, emphasis.

accentuate V. emphasize, underline, affirm, heighten.

accept V. acknowledge, receive, agree, concur, acquire.

acceptable ADJ. agreeable, pleasing, welcome, unobjectionable, average, adequate, fair.

acceptance N. agreement, assent, acquiescence, consent, approval.

accepted ADJ. orthodox, conventional, approved.

access N. admission, outburst, seizure.

accessible ADJ. approachable, open.

accessory N. assistant, helper, partner, accomplice, attachment.

accident N. misfortune, mishap, misadventure, disaster.

accidental ADJ. unintentional, inadvertent, unplanned, unexpected.

acclaim V. applaud, praise, honor.

acclimate V. adapt, harden, get used to.

acclivity N. ascent, incline, slope.

accolade N. distinction, honor.

accommodate V. oblige, adapt, conform, supply, adjust.

accompaniment N. associate, companion, attendant.

accompany V. escort, join, attend.

accomplish V. achieve, attain, perform, realize, perfect.

accomplished ADJ. practiced, skilled, finished, successful.

accomplishment N. completion, fulfillment, attainment, achievement.

accord V. concur, agree, concede, allow, permit;—N. treaty, agreement, unanimity, reconciliation.

accost V. greet, address, salute, hail.

account N. report, description, statement, explanation.

accountable ADJ. liable, responsible, amenable.

accoutrement N. outfit, dress, apparel.

accretion N. buildup, increase, accumulation, yield.

accrue V. accumulate, collect, acquire, increase, gather.

acculturate V. socialize, initiate, involve.

accumulate V. collect, gather, amass, hoard, accrue.

accumulation N. concentration, collection, amassment, store.

accumulative ADJ. additory, additive.

accuracy N. preciseness, precision, accurateness.

accurate ADJ. precise, exact, sure, certain.

accusal N. implication, accusation, incrimination.

accusation N. charge, denouncement, indictment.

accuse V. incriminate, implicate, charge, blame.

accuser N. incriminator, indicter, accusant.

accustom V. acclimatize, familiarize, habituate.

ache V. desire, feel, hurt;—N. pain.

achieve V. attain, accomplish, perform, succeed.

achievement N. accomplishment, execution, attainment, feat.

aching ADJ. painful, punishing, afflicting.

acid ADJ. sharp, sour, bitter, tart.

acknowledge V. admit, confess, declare, allow, concede.

acknowledgment N. confession, admission, recognition, acceptance.

acme N. climax, apex, zenith.

acquaint V. announce, present, inform, introduce.

acquaintance N. familiarity, experience, knowledge, friend.

acquainted ADJ. familiar, informed, knowledgeable.

acquiesce V. assent, surrender, relinquish.

acquiescence N. obedience, acceptance.

acquiescent ADJ. willing, passive.

acquire V. achieve, obtain, get, secure.

acquisition N. accomplishment, purchase, asset, possession.

acquit V. pardon, absolve, clear, prove innocent, liberate.

acrid ADJ. bitter, sour, biting.

acrimonious ADJ. resentful, bitter, malevolent.

acrimony N. malevolence, bitterness, anger, resentment.

act V. simulate, perform, execute, accomplish;— N. operation, action, performance.

acting ADJ. temporary.

action N. feat, achievement, accomplishment, activity.

activate V. energize, stimulate, actuate.

active ADJ. sharp, alert, lively, energetic.

activity N. business, exercise.

actor N. thespian, player.

actual ADJ. genuine, certain, real, sure.

actuality N. fact, reality, existence.

actually ADV. genuinely, really, truly, certainly.

actuate V. drive, activate.

acumen N. wisdom, insight, discernment, accuracy, intelligence.

acute ADJ. intense, sharp, penetrating, perceptive, precise.

adage N. proverb, saying.

adamant ADJ. stubborn, persistent, unyielding.

adamantine ADJ. stubborn, resistant, unyielding.

adapt V. conform, suit, accommodate, fit.

adaptable ADJ. adjustable, adaptive, supple.

adaptation N. adjustment, accommodation, acclimatization, conformation.

add V. enlarge, increase, augment, amplify.

addition N. supplement, increase, adjunct.

additional ADJ. further, added, more.

• **additionally** ADV. furthermore, still, also. *Furthermore, the hikers ignored the warning signs.*

additive ADJ. plus, additory, cumulative.

addled ADJ. confused, disoriented.

address V. approach, greet, acclaim, hail, speak to;—N. speech, discourse, demeanor, manners.

adept ADJ. accomplished, skillful, expert.

adequacy N. sufficiency.

• **adequate** ADJ. satisfactory, enough, sufficient, adapted, suited. *Please deliver sufficient supplies for the project.*

adhere V. attach, fasten, unite, join, bond.

adherence N. bond, support, agreement.

adhesion N. bond, traction, friction, tension.

adieu N. parting, goodbye, farewell.

adjacent ADJ. bordering, beside, neighboring, adjoining.

adjoin V. border, juxtapose, meet, touch, neighbor.

adjourn V. end, defer, terminate.

adjournment N. ending, termination.

adjudicate V. judge, decide upon.

adjunct N. complement, attachment, dependency.

• **adjust** V. regulate, adapt, organize, get used to, attune. *It may be difficult to adapt to new surroundings.*

adjustable ADJ. adaptable, plastic, versatile.

adjustment N. adaptation, variation, alteration.

adjutant N. assistant, adjunct.

ad-lib N. improvisation;—V. improvise.

administer V. govern, manage, regulate, run, administrate.

administrate V. administer, execute, carry out.

administration N. regime, government, management, direction, application.

administrator N. executive, manager, leader.

admirable ADJ. praiseworthy, worthy, wonderful, excellent.

admiration N. praise, appreciation, respect, esteem.

admire V. respect, appreciate, praise, esteem.

admirer N. fan, devotee.

admissible ADJ. worthy, passable, acceptable, approved.

admission N. confession, admittance, introduction, entry.

admit V. allow, grant, receive, induct.

admonish V. forewarn, warn, caution, reprimand.

admonishment N. warning, advice, rebuke.

admonition N. warning, rebuke.

ado N. fuss, turmoil, to-do, whirlwind.

• **adopt** V. embrace, accept, approve. *The emigrants were eager to embrace their new country's customs.*

adorable ADJ. cute, precious, lovable, sweet, wonderful.

adoration N. reverence, devotion, love, worship.

adore V. honor, love, praise, worship, idolize.

adorn V. embellish, decorate, beautify.

adroit ADJ. skillful, proficient, clever, artful.

adulate V. flatter, praise.

adulation N. praise, flattery.

adult N. mature, grownup.

adulterate V. defile, corrupt, debase.

adultery N. unfaithfulness, affair, fornication.

adumbrate V. prefigure, foreshadow, predict.

advance V. proceed, continue, progress, increase;—N. increase, advancement, continuation, headway.

advantage N. assistance, benefit, edge.

advent N. arrival, approach.

adventure N. undertaking, expedition, experiment, trip.

adventurous ADJ. exciting, venturesome, enterprising.

adversary N. enemy, opponent.

adverse ADJ. unfavorable, opposing.

adversity N. hardship, accident, misfortune, bad luck, disaster, difficulty.

advertise V. announce, promote, publicize, proclaim.

advice N. suggestion, instruction, counsel, recommendation.

• **advisable** ADJ. recommendable, counselable, expedient. *She found it most expedient to travel by train.*

advise V. recommend, inform, discuss, counsel.

adviser N. mentor, counselor, consultant.

advisory N. warning, direction, instruction, admonition.

advocate V. propose, recommend, support, promote; —N. supporter, defender.

aegis N. patronage, control, supervision.

aerate V. air, ventilate.

aerial ADJ. lofty, airy, filmy.

aesthetic ADJ. artistic, sensitive, tasteful, literary.

affable ADJ. courteous, gracious, friendly.

affair N. business, incident, liaison.

affect V. influence, change, modify, impact.

affectation N. pose, insincerity, pretention, falseness, pretense.

affected ADJ. false, pretentious, artificial.

affection N. kindness, warmth, love.

affectionate ADJ. loving, fond, doting, tender.

affiliate V. associate, join, connect, ally.

affinity N. likeness, similarity.

affirm V. declare, state, assert, propose.

affirmative ADJ. positive, favorable.

affix V. attach, fix.

affliction N. trouble, misfortune, curse, burden.

affluent ADJ. rich, wealthy, opulent.

afford V. offer, provide, manage.

affront N. provoke, insult, confront, irritate, aggravate, offend.

afraid ADJ. fearful, terrified, cowardly.

afterlife N. immortality, eternity, heaven.

aftermath N. consequence, result, effect.

afterward ADV. later, subsequently.

again ADV. anew, repeatedly, also, additionally.

age N. period, time, era;—V. mature, grow old, ripen.

aged ADJ. old, elderly, ancient, ripe.

ageless ADJ. eternal, timeless.

agency N. means, vehicle, agent, conduit.

agent N. promoter, operator, factor, means.

age-old ADJ. old, perpetual.

agglomeration N. accumulation, aggregate, total, mass.

aggravate V. irritate, anger, annoy, intensify, worsen.

aggregate N. amount, collection, total, sum, mass.

aggress V. attack, set upon.

aggression N. hostility, belligerence, aggressiveness.

aggressive ADJ. offensive, pugnacious, militant, belligerent, bold.

aggressor N. attacker, assailant.

aghast ADJ. shocked, afraid.

agile ADJ. graceful, nimble.

agility N. quickness, dexterity, nimbleness.

agitate V. perturb, shake, provoke, stir, upset.

agitation N. commotion, turbulence, turmoil, disquiet.

agonize V. suffer, afflict.

agony N. pain, torment, suffering, anguish, torture.

agree V. settle, concur, approve, join.

agreeable ADJ. charming, cooperative, friendly, pleasant.

• **agreement** N. pact, understanding, treaty, bond. *The legislators signed a pact to keep the peace.*

ahead ADJ., ADV. early, forward, before.

aid V. help, support, assist.

aide N. assistant, helper.

ail N. ill, sick; —V. worry.

ailing ADJ. sickly, ill, sick.

ailment N. disease, sickness, illness.

aim N. objective, goal, endeavor, aspiration.

aimless ADJ. purposeless, directionless.

air N. style, appearance, manner, atmosphere, firmament, sky; —V. make known.

airless ADJ. stifling, breathless, still.

airy ADJ. breezy, windy, atmospheric.

akin ADJ. related, affiliated, associated, alike.

à la mode ADJ. fashionable, modern.

alarm N. fear, terror, apprehension, panic.

alarming ADJ. fearful, frightful, terrifying.

alarmist N. terrorist, scaremonger.

alert ADJ. wakeful, wide awake, active, prepared, attentive.

alibi N. excuse, explanation, justification, pretext.

alien N. foreigner, stranger, immigrant; —ADJ. foreign.

• **alienate** V. estrange, transfer, separate, distance. *His actions may estrange some of his supporters.*

align V. line, ally.

alive ADJ. existing, living, live, animated.

all ADJ. whole, entire; —ADV. purely.

all-around ADJ. versatile, general.

allay V. calm, soothe, alleviate.

allegation N. claim, assertion, statement.

allege V. claim, assert, state, present, set forth.

allegiance N. homage, loyalty, devotion, fidelity.

alleviate V. lessen, relieve, mitigate.

alliance N. confederation, federation, union, coalition, league.

allied ADJ. unified, aligned, confederated.

allocate V. allot, distribute, give, disburse.

allot V. distribute, apportion, divide, allocate.

allow V. permit, authorize, concede, acknowledge.

allowable ADJ. permissible, bearable, endurable.

allowance N. allotment, concession, advantage, permission.

alloyed ADJ. mixed, combined, impure, adulterated.

• **all right** ADJ. fine, satisfactory; —ADV. yes, certainly. *The presentation was satisfactory but not exciting.*

allude V. refer, indicate, suggest, bring up.

allure V. draw, attract, lure, captivate.

allusive ADJ. suggestive, indicative.

ally V. align, confederate, join; —N. confederate, coalitionist, friend.

• **almost** ADV. nearly, practically, approximately, somewhat. *The stadium was nearly filled by showtime.*

alms N. donation, charity, assistance, contribution.

alone ADJ. isolated, solitary, sole, lonely.

aloof ADJ. uninterested, distant, withdrawn, separate.

already ADV. earlier, even.

- **also** ADV. as well, in addition, further, too, additionally. *The pets needed vitamins as well.*

alter V. modify, adjust, change.

alteration N. modification, adjustment, change.

alternate V. rotate, switch, interchange.

alternative N. selection, possibility, choice.

altitudinous ADJ. high, lofty.

altogether ADV. completely, wholly, entirely.

altruism N. benevolence, kindness, charity, generosity.

always ADV. perpetually, constantly, eternally.

amalgam N. mixture, blend, combination.

amass V. accumulate, gather, collect.

amateur N. beginner, novice, nonprofessional.

amateurish ADJ. unskilled, nonprofessional.

amaze V. surprise, astonish, astound.

amazement N. surprise, astonishment.

- **amazing** ADJ. surprising, astonishing, astounding, fabulous. *His astonishing feats were legendary among magicians.*

ambience N. environment, air, surroundings, atmosphere.

ambiguity N. unsureness, vagueness, equivocation.

ambiguous ADJ. unsure, unclear, obscure, vague, unexplicit.

ambition N. goal, aim, objective, desire.

ambitious ADJ. aspiring, eager, driven, motivated.

amble V. walk, stroll.

ambrosial ADJ. delicious, tasty.

ambush V. surprise, attack.

ameliorate V. improve, make better.

amenable ADJ. receptive, obedient.

amend V. better, correct, improve, fix, repair, revise.

amendment N. revision, improvement.

amends N. compensation, restitution, reparation.

amenities N. courtesies, proprieties, civilities, comforts, facilities.

amiable ADJ. pleasing, lovable, likable, gentle.

amicable ADJ. friendly, harmonious.

amiss ADV. wrong, awry.

amnesty N. forgiveness, release, reprieve.

amorous ADJ. affectionate, tender, loving.

amount N. quantity, total, sum.

amour N. love, passion, amourness.

ample ADJ. full, generous, abundant.

amplify V. increase, magnify, intensify, enlarge, expand.

amplitude N. size, bulk, scope.

amuse V. please, entertain, interest, distract.

amusement N. diversion, entertainment, distraction.

analogy N. similarity, likeness, resemblance, correspondence.

analysis N. investigation, classification, breakdown, examination, review.

• **analyze** V. investigate, examine, inspect. *This study will investigate the causes of early hair loss.*

anarchy N. disorder, rebellion, commotion, terrorism.

anathema N. hate, curse.

ancestor(s) N. descendant, predecessor, forerunner.

ancestral ADJ. hereditary, inherited.

ancestry N. descent, origin, lineage, parentage.

anchor V. fix, fasten.

ancient ADJ. archaic, old, antique, aged.

ancillary ADJ. auxiliary, supplemental.

anecdote N. narrative, story, account.

anemic ADJ. sickly, pale, unhealthy.

anesthetic N. opiate, sedative, painkiller.

angel N. innocent, sponsor, patron, seraph, archangel.

anger N. wrath, rage, resentment, exasperation.

angle N. bias, hint, point of view.

angry ADJ. upset, furious, enraged, mad.

anguish N. torment, agony, pain, distress.

angular ADJ. thin, bony, emaciated, gaunt.

animal N. beast, creature; —ADJ. physical, carnal.

animate V. enliven, inspire, invigorate, stimulate; —ADJ. alive, lively.

annals N. records, history.

annex V. add, join, append, affix; —N. addition, supplement.

annihilate V. obliterate, nullify, exterminate, destroy.

annotation N. commentary, elucidation, revision.

announce V. advertise, tell, notify, proclaim.

annoy V. irritate, harass, bother, trouble.

annul V. cancel, abolish.

anomaly N. abnormality, variation, alteration.

anonymity N. obscurity, hiddenness.

answer V. respond, reply, acknowledge, retort.

antagonism N. animosity, antipathy, opposition, conflict.

antecedent N. cause, precedent, past.

anterior ADJ. past, advance.

anticipate V. expect, forebode, foresee, forecast.

antidote N. remedy, cure, palliative.

antipathy N. hatred, repulsion, repugnance, aversion, antagonism.

antipode N. opposite, reverse, contrary.

antiquated. ADJ. old-fashioned, ancient, antique.

antique ADJ. old-fashioned, old, ancient, antiquated.

antiseptic ADJ. clean, sterile.

antithesis N. opposite, contrary.

antonymous ADJ. contrary, opposite.

anxiety N. unease, worry, anguish, disquiet, apprehension, dread.

anxious ADJ. concerned, worried, apprehensive, troubled.

anyway ADV. nevertheless, in any case.

apart ADJ. unique, solitary; —ADV. independently, aside.

apathy N. indifference, passiveness, lethargy, sluggishness.

ape V. imitate, mimic, emulate.

aperture N. hole, entrance, inlet.

apex N. point, climax, height.

aplomb N. confidence, balance.

apocalypse N. revelation, prophecy, oracle, vision.

apogee N. climax, apex, zenith.

apology N. justification, excuse, confession, acknowledgment.

apostasy N. defection, unfaithfulness, faithlessness.

apostle N. missionary, follower, disciple.

apotheosis N. exultation, transformation.

appall V. shock, horrify, frighten, dismay.

apparatus N. outfit, equipment, device.

apparel N. clothing, dress, clothes.

• **apparent** ADJ. evident, distinct, plain, obvious. *The error was evident for the auditor.*

apparition N. ghost, spirit.

appeal V. petition, request, plead, implore.

• **appearance** N. aspect, look, image, presence. *The school had the look of a rundown hotel.*

appease V. calm, soothe, pacify.

appellation N. name, moniker, title.

appendage N. branch, limb, extremity, member.

appertain V. belong, apply, concern.

appetite N. longing, craving, desire, hunger.

applaud V. praise, cheer, clap.

applause N. clapping, cheering, approval.

appliance N. device, apparatus, mechanism.

applicable ADJ. suitable, proper.

applicant N. candidate, aspirant.

application N. employment, utilization, implementation.

apply V. employ, use, utilize.

appoint V. designate, name, select, assign.

appointment N. engagement, nomination, designation.

apportion V. assign, allot, distribute, allocate, ration.

appraise V. evaluate, estimate, consider.

appreciable ADJ. perceptible, noticeable.

appreciate V. realize, comprehend, thank, prize.

appreciation N. liking, responsiveness, gratefulness, gratitude.

apprehend V. get, capture, arrest, seize.

apprehensive ADJ. uneasy, fearful, anxious, afraid.

apprise V. inform, advise, acquaint.

approach V. address, approximate.

approachable ADJ. friendly, accessible, warm, easy-going.

approbation N. praise, approval, acceptance.

appropriate V. assume, seize, take; —ADJ. proper, correct, suitable.

appropriation N. grant, usurpation, funding.

approval N. justification, endorsement, acceptance, consent.

approve V. accept, endorse, ratify, validate.

approximate V. estimate, approach; —ADJ. close, similar, inexact.

• **approximately** ADV. almost, practically, nearly, about, roughly. *She created almost one thousand costumes during her career.*

apt ADJ. suitable, appropriate, proper.

aptitude N. talent, gift, ability.

arbitrary ADJ. random, whimsical, personal, subjective.

arbitrate V. judge, adjudicate, referee, mediate.

arcane ADJ. mysterious, mystic, secret, unknown.

archaic ADJ. old-fashioned, antiquated, outdated.

arched ADJ. bend, curved, bowed, unstraight.

archetypal ADJ. typical, universal.

archetype N. original, type, model.

arctic ADJ. frigid, cold.

ardent ADJ. eager, intense, enthusiastic, passionate.

ardor N. passion, enthusiasm.

arduous ADJ. difficult, hard, burdensome, laborious.

area N. region, territory, subject, realm.

arena N. area, scene, locale, stadium.

arguable ADJ. debatable, disputable.

argue V. dispute, discuss, debate, quarrel.

• **argument** N. discussion, debate, dispute, quarrel.
  The neighbors joined in a heated discussion of the issue.

argumentative ADJ. quarrelsome, contentious, combative.

arid ADJ. dry, barren, boring.

arise V. begin, rise, get up, emerge, appear.

aristocratic ADJ. elite, noble, royal.

arm N. branch, division; —V. equip, supply.

armistice N. truce, treaty.

aroma N. fragrance, scent, smell.

around ADJ. nearby, surrounding, encircling, about.

arouse V. excite, stimulate, awaken, inspire.

arraign V. accuse, indict.

arrange V. group, distribute, place, order, assort.

arrant ADJ. shameless, flagrant.

array N. assortment, order, arrangement; clothes, dress.

arrest V. apprehend, seize, halt, capture.

arrival N. appearance, success.

arrive V. come, attain, appear, reach.

arrogance N. loftiness, disdain, presumption, pride, superiority.

arrogant ADJ. proud, insolent, disdainful, overbearing, presumptuous.

art N. craft, cunning, expertise.

artful ADJ. deft, skillful, dexterous, crafty.

article N. object, element.

articulate ADJ. vocal, eloquent, well-spoken.

artifice N. trick, art.

artificial ADJ. synthetic, manufactured, unnatural.

artistic ADJ. tasteful, creative, inventive.

artless ADJ. naive, honest, candid, unsophisticated, rustic.

ascend V. advance, progress, climb, rise.

ascendancy N. dominance, control.

ascendant ADJ. ruling, dominant.

ascension N. rise, ascent.

ascent N. rise, progress, climb, ascension.

• **ascertain** V. determine, figure out, discover, evaluate. *The researcher was unable to determine the source of the pollution.*

ascribe V. attribute, blame.

ask V. question, demand, request, appeal, interrogate.

askance ADV. skeptically, quizzically.

asleep ADJ. sleeping, dormant, inactive.

aspect N. appearance, look, expression.

asperity N. difficulty, hardship.

aspiration N. dream, ambition, hope.

aspire V. hope, try, desire, seek, crave.

assail V. revile, attack.

assault N. attack, aggression.

assemble V. collect, gather, convene.

assembly N. congress, body, congregation, gathering.

assent V. agree, allow, concur, approve.

assert V. affirm, declare, insist, state.

• **assertion** N. affirmation, statement, declaration. *His statement will certainly be challenged in court.*

assertive ADJ. emphatic, aggressive.

• **assess** V. estimate, judge, evaluate, guess, determine. *It may be difficult to estimate the extent of the damage.*

assessment N. tax, estimate, evaluation, appraisal.

assets N. resources, capacity, profits, possessions.

assiduous ADJ. applied, persistent, devoted, industrious, diligent, hardworking, ambitious.

assignment N. task, responsibility, duty.

assimilate V. habituate, conform, absorb, liken.

assist V. help, support, aid.

• **assistance** N. help, support, aid. *The town appreciated the help of nearby villages.*

assize N. law, rule.

associate V. unite, combine, ally, attach, affiliate.

assortment N. collection, melange, variety, mixture.

assuage V. relieve, pacify, make better.

• **assume** V. infer, suppose, feign, pretend, take on, appropriate. *Do not infer that the problem was his fault.*

assumption N. postulate, theory, hypothesis, conjecture, quess.

assurance N. guarantee, promise, pledge, courage, confidence.

assure V. promise, guarantee, pledge.

astonish V. surprise, startle, astound.

astound V. shock, amaze, startle, frighten, astonish.

astral ADJ. highest, grand.

astute ADJ. shrewd, sensible, reasonable, intelligent.

asylum N. home, cover, refuge.

atmosphere N. environment, flavor, air, ambience.

atrium N. court, entry, doorway, courtyard.

atrocious ADJ. outrageous, horrible, awful, unspeakable.

atrocity N. outrage, offense, horror.

attach V. secure, fasten, connect, add.

attack V. assault, violate, assail, abuse, criticize.

attain V. accomplish, obtain, gain, achieve, reach.

attempt V. endeavor, experiment; —N. effort.

attend V. frequent, serve, wait on, tend, follow, accompany.

attendant N. helper, accompaniment, servant.

• **attention** N. notice, concentration; diligence, care. *The lesson required close concentration.*

attentive ADJ. aware, mindful, observant.

attenuate V. thin, enervate, dilute.

attest V. confirm, testify, certify.

attire N. dress, apparel, clothing.

• **attitude** N. disposition, manner, view, position. *His disposition rarely changed.*

attract V. lure, draw, hold interest, appeal.

attraction N. enticement, fascination, lure, affinity.

attribute V. assign, credit, refer, ascribe; —N. characteristic, quality.

attribution N. assignment, credit, ascription.

attrition N. penitence, atonement, remorse, loss.

attune V. harmonize, adjust.

atypical ADJ. abnormal, unusual.

audacious ADJ. bold, intrepid, daring, brazen.

audacity N. arrogance, rashness, boldness, impudence.

audience N. hearing, public, listeners.

augment V. increase, intensify, add to.

augur N. prophet; —V. predict, anticipate, prophesy.

august ADJ. grand, exalted.

aurora N. dawn, dawning.

auspices N. patronage.

auspicious ADJ. opportune, favorable.

austere ADJ. severe, stern, harsh, simple, plain.

austerity N. strictness, rigor, severity, harshness.

authentic ADJ. genuine, veritable, true, legitimate, reliable.

authenticate V. validate, verify, certify, guarantee.

authenticity N. truthfulness, validity, genuineness, realness, legitimacy.

author N. dramatist, novelist, poet, originator, writer.

authoritarian ADJ. despotic, dictatorial, tyrannical, authoritative, dominant, commanding, powerful, standard, official.

authority N. rule, jurisdiction, control, supremacy, command, power.

- **authorize** V. permit, empower, allow. *Our bylaws permit only one term for the president.*

autocracy N. absolutism, dictatorship, despotism.

autograph V. sign; —N. signature.

autonomous ADJ. free, independent, self-governing.

auxiliary ADJ. assisting, secondary, supplemental.

avail V. help, serve, use, benefit.

- **available** ADJ. obtainable, ready, accessible. *They purchased the best skis obtainable.*

avarice N. greed, self-seeking.

avenge V. settle, pay back, repay, vindicate.

avenue N. way, street, road, lane.

aver V. assert, claim, avow.

average ADJ. typical, ordinary, common, undistinguished; —N. mean, median, norm.

averse ADJ. indisposed, unwilling, reluctant.

aversion N. disgust, loathing, dislike, hatred.

avert V. turn away, prevent, avoid.

avid ADJ. eager, voracious, greedy.

- **avoid** V. dodge, elude, escape, shun. *The thief was able to elude his pursuers.*

avoidance N. escape, evasion, dodging.

avow V. assert, acknowledge.

await V. expect, anticipate, remain.

awake V. alert, stimulate, arouse, wake; —ADJ. aware.

award V. honor, give, bestow, recognize.

aware ADJ. alert, mindful, sensible, cognizant.

away ADV. aside; —ADJ. distant, absent, gone.

awe N. wonder, admiration, respect, fear.

- **awful** ADJ. terrible, abominable, dreadful. *We disliked the dreadful conclusion to the movie.*

awkward ADJ. difficult, cumbersome, inconvenient, lumbering, inept.

axiom N. rule, precept, proposition.

B

babble N. chatter, gibberish, nonsense.

baby N. infant, newborn, babe.

back N. posterior, end, rear; —V. assist, support, help, endorse, finance.

backbiting ADJ. slanderous.

backbreaking ADJ. burdensome, difficult, hard.

backfire V. rebound, bounce back.

background N. history, experience.

backlog V. hoard, stockpile, reserve.

backside N. bottom, buttocks, behind.

backsliding N. lapse, slippage.

backtrack V. back up, go back.

backup N. auxiliary, supplement, substitute.

backward ADJ. behind, dull, stupid; —ADV. in reverse order.

bad ADJ. harmful, unpleasant, evil, wrong, corrupt.

badge N. decoration, emblem, cross.

badger V. provoke, harass, torment, taunt.

badly ADV. unfavorably, ineffectively, poorly.

bad-mannered ADJ. impolite, rude.

bad-tempered ADJ. ill-tempered.

baffle V. confound, outwit, frustrate, elude.

bag V. sack, catch, arrest, trap.

baggage N. suitcases, pack, equipment, luggage.

bail N. bond, deposit, surety.

bait V. entice, captivate, lure, tease, pester.

bake V. burn, toast, cook.

balance N. stability, proportion, equilibrium.

balanced ADJ. sane, fair.

bald ADJ. bare, hairless.

bald-faced ADJ. shameless, audacious.

baleful ADJ. detrimental, harmful, injurious, destructive.

balk V. stop, hesitate, check.

balloon V. enlarge, swell, bulge.

balmy ADJ. gentle, soothing, mild.

ban V. prohibit, outlaw, forbid, censor.

banal ADJ. overused, trite, insipid.

band N. association, group, gang.

bandage N. dress, wrapping, repair.

bandy V. exchange, give back.

bane N. poison, curse, ruin.

bang V. blow, blast, slam, hit.

banish V. expel, dismiss, deport, ostracize.

bank N. shore, embankment.

bankroll V. finance, support, back.

bankrupt ADJ. ruined, broke.

banner N. flag, colors, pennant.

banquet N. feast, meal, entertainment.

bantam ADJ. tiny, small, dainty, feisty.

banter V. chatter, joke, humor, tease.

baptize V. bless, consecrate, christen.

bar N. barricade, hindrance, barrier, obstacle; saloon, café, lounge; —V. prevent, impede, stop, hinder.

barbarian N. brute, ruffian, savage.

bard N. poet, storyteller, muse, author.

bare ADJ. uncovered, naked, nude, empty, unfurnished, barren, plain, scarce.

• **barely** ADV. hardly, scarcely, almost, nearly, approximately, just. *He felt hardly any pain during the procedure.*

bargain N. arrangement, deal, contract, agreement.

bark V. snap, crack, yelp.

baroque ADJ. elaborate, embellished, ornate.

barrage N. bombardment, shower, burst.

barren ADJ. bare, sterile, fruitless, unproductive, empty, futile.

barricade N. fence, barrier, wall, obstacle.

basal ADJ. radical, elementary.

base ADJ. worthless, vile, corrupt, low; —N. theme, basis, headquarters, complex, station.

baseless ADJ. unjustifiable, groundless, unfounded, empty.

bash N. party, blast; —V. hit.

bashful ADJ. shy, modest, timid.

basic ADJ. essential, fundamental, primary, elementary.

- **basically** ADV. essentially, mainly, chiefly, fundamentally. *The company was essentially a one-person operation.*

basin N. depression, watershed, sink, tub.

basis N. foundation, ground, base, justification.

bask V. luxuriate, sun, loaf, enjoy.

bass N. low sound, deep tone.

bastard ADJ. illegitimate.

baste V. moisten; beat, thrash; sew.

batch N. set, bunch, cluster.

bate V. subside, return.

bathos N. sentimentality, foolishness.

batter V. hit, strike, pummel.

battle N. combat, warfare, struggle, war.

batty ADJ. insane, crazy.

bawd N. prostitute, whore.

bay N. cove, harbor, gulf.

be V. exist, subsist, live.

beak N. bill, nose.

beam N. timber, girder; —V. gleam, glow, shine, glisten.

bear V. carry, transport, support, endure, tolerate, stand.

bearing N. behavior, carriage, posture, reference, connection.

beast N. monster, fiend, brute, animal.

beat V. batter, hit, strike, hammer, defeat, surpass.

beatitude N. happiness, blessing.

beau N. suitor, admirer, boyfriend, lover.

- **beautiful** ADJ. lovely, attractive, pretty, gorgeous, fair, handsome. *We admired the lovely roses.*

beauty N. attractiveness, loveliness.

beckon V. call, summon, signal.

become V. change, grow, suit, come to be.

becoming ADJ. proper, fitting, suitable, decent.

bedazzle V. daze, amaze, stun.

bedeck V. adorn, decorate.

bedevil V. besiege, annoy.

bedraggled ADJ. shabby, disheveled.

befall V. chance, happen.

befit V. suit, fit.

before ADJ. prior, earlier, ahead; —ADV. sooner.

befuddle V. daze, stun, confuse.

beg V. plead, petition, implore, entreat, supplicate.

beget V. father, propagate.

beggar N. homeless person, poor person, needy person, pauper, supplicant.

- **begin** V. initiate, start, commence. *She wanted to initiate her business plans as soon as possible.*

beginner N. novice, apprentice, amateur, initiate.

beginning N. outset, source, origin, inception, start.

begrudge V. envy, resent.

beguile V. deceive, fool.

behave V. act, comport.

- **behavior** N. action, manners, comportment, conduct, attitude, demeanor. *Judge his values by his action.*

behemoth N. giant, leviathan.

behind ADJ., ADV. in back of, slow, late; —N. bottom.

behold V. look at, see, perceive.

being N. essence, nature, existence, actuality, thing.

belated ADJ. late, overdue.

belch V. burp, erupt.

belie V. refute, distort.

belief N. opinion, conviction, persuasion.

believable ADJ. plausible, credible.

- **believe** V. accept, trust, credit, feel, deem. *They are willing to accept his explanation.*

belittle V. minimize, discredit, humiliate, diminish.

bellicose ADJ. warlike, belligerent, military.

belligerence N. hostility, aggression, bellicosity.

bellow V. scream, roar, yell, shout.

belly N. stomach, abdomen; —V. bulge, swell.

- **belong** V. pertain, fit, appertain, have to do with. *These files pertain to the Smith case.*

beloved ADJ. favorite, darling, loved, dear.

belt N. area; —V. hit, strike.

bemuse V. daze, amaze, mesmerize.

benchmark N. standard, criterion, gauge.

bend V. curve, turn, bow, deflect, submit, yield.

benediction N. grace, blessing.

benefaction N. donation, benevolence, contribution.

benefactor N. patron, donor, backer.

beneficence N. donation, benevolence, contribution.

• **beneficial** ADJ. helpful, useful, good, favorable. *Her expertise proved helpful to our efforts.*

benefit N. advantage, profit, favor, service.

benevolence N. kindness, tenderness, humanity, charity.

benign ADJ. harmless, favorable, benevolent.

bent ADJ. curved, crooked, arched.

bequeath V. give to, leave, hand down.

berate V. bawl out, criticize.

bereave V. deprive, take away, withdraw.

berth N. place, position.

beseech V. implore, ask, beg, appeal.

beset V. attack, annoy, surround.

• **besides** ADV. additionally, furthermore, moreover, in addition. *In addition, the team needed new uniforms.*

besiege V. blockage, beset, harass, surround.

best ADJ. optimal, optimum, largest; —N. elite.

bestial ADJ. fierce, animalistic.

bestow V. award, give, present, donate.

bet V. gamble, wager, stake.

betray V. expose, reveal, be treacherous.

betrothal N. engagement, promise.

better ADJ. superior, preferable.

bevel N. slant, angle, slope, inclination.

beverage N. drink, libation.

bevy N. group, assembly, collection.

beware V. look out, be cautious, take care, be careful.

bewilder V. puzzle, mystify, confuse.

bewitch V. captivate, charm, enchant, dazzle.

bias N. prejudice, inclination, partiality.

bicker V. dispute, argue, quarrel.

bid V. offer, propose, direct, order; —N. proposal, invitation, offer.

bide V. remain, pause, delay.

big ADJ. immense, large, enormous, important, gigantic, huge.

bigotry N. prejudice, intolerance, bias.

bill N. charge, invoice, account.

binary ADJ. double, polar.

bind V. fasten, tie, affix, commit.

binge N. rampage, orgy, spree.

birth N. ancestry, onset, beginning, childbirth, labor, start.

birthright N. right, prerogative, inheritance, legacy.

bit N. fragment, scrap, particle.

bite V. chew, eat, sting; —N. mouthful, morsel, snack.

biting ADJ. acidic, pungent, bitter, cutting.

bitter ADJ. acidic, acrid, sour, biting.

• **bizarre** ADJ. fantastic, eccentric, strange, unusual. *His eccentric clothing aroused many questions.*

black ADJ. dark, dirty, evil, gloomy, ebony, jet.

blacken V. stain, dirty, smear, tarnish, darken.

blade N. edge, knife.

• **blame** V. condemn, criticize, reprove, accuse, censure. *Do not condemn the person before the trial.*

blameless ADJ. innocent, exemplary.

blanched ADJ. pale, white.

bland ADJ. neutral, plain, gentle.

blank ADJ. vacant, bare, void, expressionless.

blare V. scream, yell, glare.

blasphemy N. sacrilege, profanity.

blast N. explosion, detonation, blowout.

blatant ADJ. shameless, obvious, brazen, flagrant.

blaze N. inferno, fire, flame.

bleach V. whiten, pale.

bleary ADJ. unclear, exhausted.

bleed V. ooze, flow from, exude.

blemish N. stain, flaw, detect, mark, spot.

blend V. mix, combine, harmonize.

bless V. thank, sanctify.

blight N. disease, affliction, sickness; —V. destroy, damage, ruin.

blind ADJ. sightless, unseeing, dull, unperceptive.

blink V., N. wink, twinkle, flicker, flash.

blithe ADJ. jolly, happy, joyful, animated, gay.

blockade V. block, attack; —n. barrier, wall.

blockhead N. dullard, idiot, jerk, dope.

blond ADJ. fair, flaxen.

blood N. bloodshed, gore, murder; heritage, ancestry.

bloodcurdling ADJ. horrible, frightening, awful.

bloodless ADJ. pale, insensitive.

bloodline N. lineage, ancestry.

bloodshed N. massacre, slaughter, warfare.

bloodstained ADJ. bloody, smeared.

bloody ADJ. bloodstained, murderous, cruel.

bloom V. blossom, flower.

blossom V. flower, flourish, bloom.

blot V. stain, smear, spot, blemish, flaw.

blow V. slap, hit, shock, stroke; explode, inflate.

blowhard N. braggart, boaster.

blowout N. explosion, blast.

blowup N. outburst, blast.

bludgeon V. intimidate, beat, pummel, assault.

blue ADJ. azure; depressed, unhappy, sad, melancholic.

blue-blooded ADJ. noble, aristocratic, royal.

blueprint N. design, plan.

blues N. gloom, depression.

bluff N. cliff, escarpment; —V. ruse, challenge; —ADJ. impolite, bold, rude, frank, outspoken, open.

blunder N. error, mistake, faux pas.

blunt ADJ. dull, direct, impolite, rude.

blur V. dim, obscure, stain, smudge.

blurt V. exclaim, shout.

blush V. color, redden.

board V. harbor, take, lodge.

boast V. brag, exaggerate.

bodily ADJ. personal, physical, corporal.

body N. group, assembly, quantity; cadaver, corpse.

boggle V. stagger, bewilder, surprise.

boil V. bubble, simmer, stew, cook.

boisterous ADJ. vociferous, noisy, loud, rowdy.

bold ADJ. fearless, brave, daring.

bold-faced ADJ. impudent, shameless.

bolster V. support, sustain, help.

bombardment N. barrage, bombing.

bombastic ADJ. sonorous, rhetorical, overdone.

bond N. tie, attachment, convenant, commitment, contract.

bonny ADJ. good, beautiful.

bonus N. gift, reward, bounty.

booby trap N. pitfall, trap, lair.

book N. work, publication, text, novel, tome.

bookish ADJ. studious, pedantic, scholarly.

boom N. rumble, blast, thunder, roar, prosperity.

boon N. advantage, fortune, luck, benevolence.

boor N. barbarian, philistine, boob, clown.

boost V. promote, elevate, lift, increase.

boot V. eject, dismiss.

booty N. plunder, reward, treasure, bounty.

bop V. blow, hit.

border N. edge, periphery, frontier, boundary, limit.

• **bore** V. tire, weary, fatigue; drill, perforate. *An interminable lecture can tire even the most interested student.*

boredom N. ennui, tedium, tiredness.

bosom N. heart, chest, breast, feelings.

boss N. director, employer, supervisor, chief, leader.

botch V. fumble, wreck, ruin, mix up, mess up.

bother V. disturb, irritate, annoy.

bottom N. base, depth; —ADJ. lowest, undermost.

bounce V. rebound, jump, spring, eject.

bound N. bounce, limit, boundary, border; —ADJ. destined, compelled.

boundary N. border, frontier, limit, outline.

bountiful ADJ. plentiful, generous, fulsome.

bouquet N. fragrance, compliment, nosegay.

bout N. contest, match, fight.

bow V. bend, stoop, yield, give in, succumb.

bowdlerize V. censor, edit, revise.

box N. predicament, flap; carton, crate.

boy N. youngster, kid, youth.

boycott V. blackball, strike, avoid.

boyfriend N. beau, friend, male companion, significant other.

brace V. support, crutch, prop.

bracket N. class, category; support, prop.

brag V. boast, exaggerate.

braggart N. bragger, blowhard.

brain N. mind, intelligence, sense, intellect.

brainstorm N. inspiration, idea.

branch N. division, part, limb, offshoot.

brand N. manufacture, kind, trademark; —V. mark, stamp.

brandish V. flourish, display.

brash ADJ. tactless, presumptuous, brazen.

brave ADJ. fearless, heroic, brave-hearted, steadfast, courageous, valiant.

brawl N. riot, dispute, disturbance, fight.

brawn N. strength, muscle.

brazen ADJ. shameless, impudent, rude, bold.

breach V. break, rupture, transgress, trespass.

bread N. food, living, money.

breadth N. expanse, width.

break V. shatter, smash, fracture, split; disobey, collapse; —N. breach, interruption.

breakable ADJ. fragile, delicate.

breakage N. destruction, wreckage, damage.

breakdown N. failure, collapse, decay; analysis.

breakneck ADJ. fast, speedy, quick.

breakout N. escape, flight, getaway.

breast N. heart, chest, bosom.

breath N. inhalation, respiration, exhalation.

breathe V. respire, inhale, exhale.

breathless ADJ. airless, amazed.

breed V. father, create, conceive, bear, propagate.

breeze N. wind, air, zephyr.

bribe N. payoff, inducement.

bridal N. wedding, marriage.

bridle V. restraint, control, check.

- **brief** ADJ. temporary, short, concise, succinct. *A temporary electrical outage delayed our departure.*

bright ADJ. shining, brilliant, radiant, luminous.

- **brilliant** ADJ. radiant, bright, shining; gifted, intelligent, talented. *The radiant diamond brought gasps of admiration from onlookers.*

brim N. margin, border, edge, lip.

brimming ADJ. full, bordering, verging.

bring V. carry, take, bear; cause.

brink N. verge, limit, border, edge.

brisk ADJ. energetic, lively, agile.

bristle V. teem, anger.

brittle ADJ. delicate, thin, fragile, weak, breakable.

broach V. introduce, open, raise, bring up, put forth.

broad ADJ. wide, large, sizable, considerable, expansive, liberal, progressive, open-minded.

broad-minded ADJ. liberal, unprejudiced, tolerant, open-minded.

broil V. burn, cook.

broke ADJ. poor, impoverished.

broken-down ADJ. shabby, old.

broker N. go-between, agent.

bromide N. cliché, saying.

brood N. offspring, young, litter; —V. worry, dwell on.

brook N. branch; stream, creek.

brotherhood N. friendship, fellowship, community, camaraderie.

browbeat V. intimidate, threaten.

browse V. scan, skim, glance at.

bruise V. wound, injure.

bruit V. noise, advertise.

brush V. shave, skim, graze; whisk, broom, scrub.

brusque ADJ. abrupt, rough, blunt, curt.

brutal ADJ. savage, barbaric, mean, cruel.

brutalize V. attack, injure.

buckle V. clasp, fasten; collapse, give way, fail, yield.

bucolic ADJ. rustic, country.

buddy N. associate, friend, pal, fellow.

budget N. quantity, projection, money, allowance.

buffet N. cabinet, counter, sideboard; —V. beat, slap, hit.

bug N. germ, defect; —V. annoy, irritate, bother.

• **build** V. assemble, construct, erect, make. *The children learned to assemble their own playhouse.*

building N. edifice, house, structure.

built-in ADJ. constituent, incorporated, inherent, innate, natural.

bulge N. lump, swelling, enlargement; —V. swell, balloon, protrude.

bulk N. magnitude, quantity, size, volume.

bulky ADJ. huge, massive, oversized, clumsy, awkward.

bull N. nonsense, stupidity.

bulldoze V. push, intimidate.

bullheaded ADJ. obstinate, stubborn, difficult.

bully V. intimidate, harass; —N. persecutor, heckler, tormentor.

bumbling ADJ. unskillful, awkward, clumsy.

bump V. hit, strike, knock, collide.

• **bunch** N. group, crowd, cluster, bundle. *A group of teenagers stood in line for tickets.*

bundle N. packet; —V. bunch, package, group.

bungle V. botch, mess up.

buoyant ADJ. floating, airy, cheerful, bright, gay, lighthearted.

burden V. worry, trouble, load, laden.

burgeon V. rise, bloom.

burglarize V. rob, thieve, break in.

burial N. interment, entombment, funeral.

burlesque N. mockery, satire.

burn V. blaze, blame, fire, bake.

burning ADJ. pressing, imperative; blazing, afire.

burnish V. gloss, polish, buff.

burrow N. hole, den, tunnel.

burst V. explode, pop, blow up.

bursting ADJ. eager, full, exploding.

bury V. conceal, cover, hide, inter.

- **business** N. firm, company, concern, corporation. *Her firm offered excellent health benefits.*

businesslike ADJ. efficient, serious, methodical.

businessperson N. dealer, agent, employee, manager.

bust V. break, ruin, arrest; —N. failure; statue, chest, bosom.

bustle V. hurry, rush, stir.

- **busy** ADJ. hardworking, engaged, occupied, crowded. *The hardworking weavers produced six carpets per week.*

busybody N. snoop, gossip, interloper, intruder.

but ADV. still, however, moreover, besides, nevertheless, though; —CONJ. yet, unless, except, notwithstanding.

butcher V. annihilate, destroy, murder.

butt N. end, bottom; —V. thrust, adjoin.

buy V. obtain, purchase, acquire, believe.

buzz N. gossip, hum.

by ADJ. close to, near.

bygone ADJ. old-fashioned, passé.

bypass V. skirt, avoid, go around.

by-product N. derivative, result, outcome.

byword N. motto, proverb, slogan.

C

cache V. hide, conceal; —N. storehouse, stockroom.

cackle V. laugh, shout, exclaim, tattle.

cacophonous ADJ. noisy, inharmonious.

cadaver N. body, corpse.

cadence N. rhythm, speed, beat.

cage V. enclose, trap.

cajole V. lure, beguile, humor, coax.

calamity N. disaster, mishap, misfortune, distress.

calculate V. figure, estimate, consider, weigh, compute.

calendar N. schedule, program.

call V. shout, exclaim, address, name, summon.

callous ADJ. indifferent, insensible, unfeeling, hard.

calm ADJ. collected, reserved, tranquil, quiet, sedate.

calumniate V. libel, slander, defame, lie.

camouflage V. disguise, cover, hide.

can V. know how to, dismiss, preserve.

cancel V. erase, delete, annul, abolish.

candid ADJ. frank, honest, truthful, simple, straightforward.

candidate N. applicant, contestant, aspirant, hopeful.

candy N. sweets, confection.

cane N. stick, pole, club, rod, staff.

canny ADJ. sharp, economical.

canon N. regulation, standard, precept, rule, law.

cant N. jargon, argot.

cap V., N. cover, top.

- **capable** ADJ. skilled, competent, able. *One worker proved more skilled than the other.*

capacious ADJ. full, roomy.

- **capacity** N. content, aptitude, capability, faculty, talent. *The factory had the capability of doubling its production.*

caper N. adventure, antic, prank, gambol.

capital ADJ. important, best, principal, first; —N. money, principal, property.

capitalize V. finance, benefit.

capitulate V. succumb, give in to.

caprice N. fancy, whim.

capricious ADJ. fanciful, whimsical, odd, inconstant, inconsistent.

captain N. leader, supervisor, director, commander.

captivate V. enthrall, charm, fascinate, enchant.

capture V. seize, catch, trap, take, apprehend.

carcass N. body, cadaver.

cardinal ADJ. fundamental, capital, principal, important, essential.

care N. anxiety, worry, concern, attention, heed.

- **careful** ADJ. vigilant, cautious, concerned, meticulous. *It pays to remain vigilant after dark.*

  careless ADJ. unthoughtful, reckless, negligent, thoughtless, uncaring.

  caress V. kiss, embrace, hug.

  carnage N. massacre, destruction, slaughter, havoc.

  carnal ADJ. worldly, concupiscent, lascivious, physical.

  carouse V. revel, celebrate, party.

  carp V. quibble, scold, nag, berate.

  carry V. move, transfer, bear, bring.

  case N. situation, circumstance, occurrence, instance, example, condition.

  cast V. throw, direct, toss, pitch.

  castigate V. call down.

  castrate V. sterilize, emasculate.

- **casual** ADJ. careless, relaxed, negligent, unintentional. *His careless dress was inappropriate for the interview.*

  casualty N. disaster; injured, wounded, victim, dead.

  cataclysm N. flood, disaster, revolution.

  catalyst N. leavening, yeast, accelerator.

  catastrophe N. disaster, calamity, cataclysm, accident.

  catch V. capture, grasp, seize, snare, trap.

  categorical ADJ. definite.

categorize V. class, assort, organize.

cater to V. humor, baby.

catharsis N. cleansing, purification, purge.

- **cause** N. origin, reason, motive, determinant, necessity, justification. *The origin of the problem lay in his eating habits.*

caustic ADJ. harsh, disagreeable, malicious, mean, spiteful.

caution N. care, acumen, foresight, wariness.

cave N. hole, cavern, grotto.

caveat N. warning.

cavil V. quibble, argue, dispute.

cavity N. depression, cave, hollow, opening.

cavort V. gambol, revel.

cease V. stop, terminate, end, quit, desist, discontinue.

ceaseless ADJ. neverending, continual.

celebrate V. honor, glorify, observe, commemorate.

celebrity N. star, idol, fame.

celestial ADJ. heavenly, angelic, unearthly, ethereal.

censor V. screen, suppress, edit, delete, ban.

censure V. deplore, blame, disapprove, criticize.

center N. middle, core, nucleus, heart.

central ADJ. principal, dominant, fundamental, essential, focal, middle.

cerebral ADJ. mental, intellectual.

ceremony N. service, ritual, rite.

certain ADJ. sure, assured, confident, reliable, positive.

- **certainly** ADV. absolutely, definitely, surely. *The leader is absolutely committed to the new program.*

certainty N. actuality, fact, sureness, truth.

certify V. authenticate, verify, validate, affirm, substantiate, guarantee.

chagrin N. embarrassment, irritation, annoyance, shame.

chain N. series, sequence, row, succession.

- **challenge** N. contest, rival, defiance, obstacle. *The two managers looked upon the job as a contest.*

chance N. hazard, luck, fortune, fortuity, risk, opportunity.

- **change** V. modify, vary, alter, exchange; —N. alteration, modification, variation. *We can modify the design to reduce friction.*

chant N. singing, song, hymn.

chaotic ADJ. confusing, tumultuous, anomalous.

character N. disposition, nature, personality, honesty, integrity, reference, reputation.

characterize V. distinguish, call.

charge V. accuse, blame, indict, attack, price, sell for.

charisma N. attraction, charm, allure, influence.

charity N. giving, generosity, beneficence, philanthropy.

charm V. enchant, enthrall, beguile, please, fascinate.

charming ADJ. captivating, delightful, ravishing, fascinating, pleasing.

chart N., V. diagram, map, plan.

chary ADJ. wary, economical.

chase V. pursue, seek, track, stalk, hunt.

chaste ADJ. simple, innocent, pure, neat, uncorrupted.

chastise V. punish, discipline, correct, reprimand.

chastity N. purity, virtue, decency, modesty.

chatter V. converse, talk, rattle, babble, gab.

cheap ADJ. inexpensive, common, shabby, inferior.

check V. stop, examine, hinder, moderate.

cheer N. happiness, cheerfulness, joy, merriment, gaiety; —V. comfort, gladden.

chew V. bite, nibble, masticate.

chide V. call down, scold, admonish, rebuke, criticize.

chief ADJ. principal, paramount, essential, first; —N. director, leader, boss.

child N. youngster, juvenile, kid, youth, minor.

childish ADJ. immature, infantile, childlike.

childlike ADJ. babyish, immature, childish.

chilly ADJ. cool, cold.

chime V. ring, clang, peal; —N. alarm, buzzer, bell.

chivalrous ADJ. gallant, brave, valiant, heroic, courteous.

choice N. selection, preference, alternative, option; —ADJ. superior, exceptional, select.

choke V. gag, strangle, suffocate, stifle.

choose V. pick, select, elect, decide upon.

chop V. cut, mince, hew.

chore N. work, task, duty.

chronic ADJ. lingering, persistent, continuing, habitual, sustained.

chuckle V. laugh, giggle, snicker.

church N. faith, temple, synagogue, religion, theology.

churn V. boil, agitate.

circle N. disk, ring, society, clique, class.

circuit N. revolution, circle, course, orbit.

circumscribe V. confine, limit, enclose, bound.

circumspect ADJ. heedful, careful, observant, discreet.

circumstance N. situation, incident, occurrence, happening, fact.

cite V. name, summon, call, quote, mention.

citizen N. native, subject, dweller, inhabitant, resident.

city N. municipality, town, village, urban setting.

civic ADJ. public, civil, municipal.

civil ADJ. public, courteous, gracious, polite.

civilization N. culture, society.

• **claim** V. contend, assert, maintain, declare. *They contend that illness is hereditary.*

clamor N. shouting, noise, uproar, roar.

clan N. family, group.

• **clarify** V. define, explain, make clear, elucidate, illuminate. *Please define your key terms.*

clasp V. hold, clutch, hug, embrace; —N. buckle, hook.

class N. rank, order, classification, group, grade.

classic ADJ. vintage, typical, elegant, simple, refined.

clean ADJ. cleansed, purified, stainless, pure.

clear ADJ. lucid, transparent, vivid, bright, apparent, obvious, definite, straightforward.

clergyman N. preacher, priest, chaplain, rabbi.

clever ADJ. bright, capable, skillful, sharp, keen, quick.

click V. snap, succeed, relate.

climate N. aura, atmosphere, environment.

climax N. peak, summit, culmination, pinnacle.

climb V. ascend, scale, rise.

clock V. time; —N. watch, chronometer.

close ADJ. near, immediate, nearby, adjoining, adjacent, attached; —V. shut, conclude, finish, terminate, end.

clothe V. dress, robe, cloak.

cloudy ADJ. indefinite, blurred, dim, obscure, overcast, sunless, gloomy.

clumsy ADJ. awkward, ungainly, inept, ungraceful.

clutch V. hold, grasp, embrace, seize.

clutter N. mess, disorder, chaos.

coarse ADJ. crude, rough, vulgar, unrefined.

coax V. cajole, entice, flatter, invite.

coerce V. force, hijack.

cogent ADJ. valid, powerful, sound, persuasive.

cogitate V. reason, consider, ponder, think.

cognizant ADJ. aware, alert.

cohere V. bond, join, conform.

cohort N. follower, associate.

coincide V. agree, correspond, synchronize, match, concur.

cold ADJ. frigid, cool, distant, aloof, reserved, passionless.

collaborate V. concur, cooperate, unite, conspire.

collapse V. faint, give way, fail, break in.

collect V. obtain, summon, receive, assemble, compose.

collide V. crash, hit, bump.

colloquial ADJ. conversational, informal, familiar.

color N. tone, tint, hue.

colorful ADJ. vivid, impressive, bright, picturesque.

colossal ADJ. gigantic, enormous, giant, huge, immense.

comb V. brush, scour.

combat N. contest, battle, fight, struggle.

• **combination** N. mixing, mixture, blend, association, union. *A mixing of three coffee types produced the most savory blend.*

combine V. mix, join, blend, connect.

come V. advance, near, proceed, approach.

comfort V. help, support, encourage, console.

comical ADJ. laughable, amusing, funny, humorous.

command V. direct, order, instruct, lead.

commemorate V. memorialize, celebrate, observe.

commence V. start, begin, initiate, dawn.

commend V. approve, praise, compliment, extol.

commend N. remark, explanation, observation; —V. observe, note, remark.

commiserate V. feel, sympathize, empathize.

commit V. perform, carry out, entrust, authorize, delegate.

• **common** ADJ. mutual, shared, joined, familiar, ordinary, everyday, average, normal, acceptable, inferior. *Our mutual interests are best served by cooperation.*

communal ADJ. common, joint, public, shared.

communicable ADJ. contagious, infectious, catching.

• **communicate** V. relate, express, convey, impart, tell, disclose. *The adventurer was eager to relate his tale.*

community N. public, society, city, town, village.

compact ADJ. packed, compressed, thick, tight; —N. bargain, agreement, pact; —V. consolidate, combine, compress.

companion N. friend, partner, colleague, associate.

• **company** N. establishment, business, firm, visitor, guest, companionship, assembly, group. *The establishment will open for business next week.*

compare V. match, contrast, liken.

compassion N. pity, sympathy, kindness, tenderness.

compensate V. balance, recompense, reimburse, pay.

• **compete** V. contend, contest, rival, oppose. *The athletes will contend for the prize.*

competent ADJ. able, skilled, qualified, sufficient.

competitor N. opponent, contender, rival, contestant.

complacent ADJ. lazy, uncaring, laid back, assured, satisfied, content.

complain V. protest, fret, grumble, gripe.

complaisant ADJ. obliging, amiable.

complement N. supplement, completion, accompaniment.

complete ADJ. thorough, whole, finished, entire; —V. accomplish, effect, realize, conclude.

complex ADJ. compound, involved, complicated, intricate, perplexing.

compliant ADJ. obedient, obliging.

compliment V. praise, recommend, felicitate, congratulate.

component N. element, part, piece.

compose V. create, write, make, form.

composite ADJ. complex; —N. combination, mixture.

• **comprehend** V. grasp, understand, perceive, know. *He failed to grasp the importance of the message.*

compress V. squeeze, crowd, reduce, contract.

comprise V. make up, contain, constitute, include, involve.

compromise N. conciliation, settlement, agreement; —V. agree, concede, conciliate.

• **compute** V. count, calculate, add, figure. *Please count the number of envelopes needed for the mailing.*

comrade N. associate, friend, companion.

concave ADJ. hollow, sunken.

conceal V. cover, hide, cache.

concede V. compromise, acknowledge, admit, give in, yield.

conceit N. egotism, vanity, self-esteem, pride.

• **conceive** V. imagine, understand, invent, grasp. *Can you imagine a wingless airplane?*

concentrate V. condense, focus, converge.

• **concept** N. idea, theory, thought. *Her idea led to the eventual vaccine.*

- **concern** N. interest, regard, worry, anxiety. *He won friends by showing interest in them.*

concise ADJ. brief, condensed, pointed, short.

conclude V. terminate, end, finish, settle.

concrete ADJ. real, tangible, solid, particular.

condemn V. denounce, convict, sentence, reprobate.

condense V. thicken, compact, shorten.

- **condition** N. status, state, position, situation, necessity, requirement. *The status of the space craft will not be known for another hour.*

condone V. forgive, pardon, allow, excuse.

conduct V. manage, direct, guide, regulate; —N. demeanor, behavior, attitude.

confederate N. ally, associate; —V. join, unite.

confer V. talk, consult, discuss, deliberate, donate, bestow.

confide V. share, entrust, whisper.

confidential ADJ. private, classified, restricted, intimate.

confine V. bound, limit, imprison, restrict.

confirm V. substantiate, corroborate, validate, approve, affirm.

confiscate V. seize, appropriate, take.

conflict N. clash, friction, contention, difficulty.

conform V. submit, yield, follow, agree.

confound V. confuse, perplex, bewilder, puzzle, baffle.

confront V. encounter, face, accost.

- **confuse** V. bewilder, confound, perturb, mistake, mix up. *The evidence may bewilder even the most expert detective.*

congenial ADJ. gracious, friendly, agreeable, grateful.

congest V. fill, crowd, choke, clog.

conjecture N. guess, speculation, presumption, hypothesis, theory.

- **connect** V. attach, associate, relate, unite. *Be sure to attach the safety latch.*

connive V. plot, plan.

conquer V. gain, triumph, overcome, defeat.

- **conscious** ADJ. aware, sensible, awake, purposeful, intentional. *He was aware of his important responsibility.*

consecrate V. sanctify, devote.

consecutive ADJ. sequential, next, succeeding, subsequent, ensuing.

consensus N. unanimity, opinion, group feeling.

consent N. permission, acceptance, agreement; —V. permit, allow, agree.

- **consequence** N. result, impact, effect, importance, significance. *As a result of her actions, the child was saved.*

conservative ADJ. right-wing, orthodox, reactionary, conventional, traditional.

conserve V. preserve, save, keep, retain.

- **consider** V. reflect upon, study, deliberate,

inspect, examine. *I hope you will study your choices more thoroughly.*

- **considerable** ADJ. much, important, big, great, noteworthy, worthwhile. *There was much work to be done.*

- **consideration** N. kindness, thoughtfulness, esteem, empathy; payment, deposit. *Her kindness won many friends for the company.*

consist V. lie, reside, dwell, exist.

- **consistent** ADJ. invariable, constant, unchanging, same. *The scientists reached invariable results, no matter what the temperature.*

consolation N. comfort, solace, sympathy.

conspicuous ADJ. prominent, obvious, noticeable, visible.

constant ADJ. stable, invariable, steady, permanent.

constitute V. compose, form, create, organize, appoint, authorize, delegate.

construct V. make, build, form, erect, produce.

construe V. interpret, explain, translate.

consult V. discuss, confer.

consume V. devour, waste, exhaust, destroy, annihilate.

contact N. meeting, contingence, touch; —V. reach, touch.

contagious ADJ. communicable, catching, spreading.

contain V. hold, embody, encompass, compose, have.

contaminate V. poison, spoil, dirty, pollute.

contemplate V. ponder, consider, reflect, meditate.

contemporary ADJ. concurrent, coexistent, existing, related, simultaneous, present.

contempt N. disrespect, hatred, derision, scorn.

contend V. compete, argue, oppose, fright.

contest N. fight, dispute, challenge, competition; —V. oppose, challenge, dispute.

continual ADJ. eternal, timeless, unending, everlasting.

continue V. go on, resume, sustain, persist, advance, proceed.

contract V. shorten, diminish, condense, reduce; —N. agreement, promise, covenant.

contradict V. dispute, resist, oppose, deny.

contrary ADJ. opposite, conflicting, adverse, antagonistic.

contrast V. differentiate, differ, distinguish; —N. distinction, difference, incongruity.

contribute V. donate, share, give, help.

- **control** N. authority, management, administration, command; —V. direct, manage, administer, dominate, rule. *The student president had the authority to hire several assistants.*

controversy N. quarrel, dispute, argument.

convene V. assemble, meet.

- **convenient** ADJ. accessible, handy, available. *The right tools were easily accessible for the job.*

convention N. meeting, conference, assembly.

conventional ADJ. accepted, customary, usual, conforming.

conversation N. talk, discussion, chat, chatter, intercourse, dialogue.

converse V. talk, speak, visit.

convert V. transform, transfigure, change, alter, modify.

convey V. express, communicate, impart, transfer, transmit.

conviction N. sureness, belief, position.

convince V. persuade, satisfy, assure.

cook V. prepare, boil, broil, fry, bake.

cool ADJ. calm, nonchalant, distant, reserved, cold, remote.

• **cooperate** V. collaborate, unite, help, combine.
The writers decided to collaborate on the project.

coordinate V. match, harmonize, adapt, organize.

copy N. imitation, simulation, reproduction, duplicate; —V. simulate, reproduce, duplicate.

cordial ADJ. polite, gracious, friendly, amiable.

correct V. edit, amend, rectify; —ADJ. right, accurate, proper, respectable, appropriate.

correlate V. associate, relate, compare.

correspond V. compare, agree, coincide.

corroborate V. certify, confirm, prove, affirm.

corrupt ADJ. unscrupulous, perverse, debased, low, degenerate, dishonest.

cost N. value, price, charge, expense, sacrifice.

counsel V. advise, guide, admonish, inform.

count V. calculate, number, compute, enumerate.

counterfeit ADJ. fraudulent, false, bogus, phony.

country N. state, territory; —ADJ. provincial, rustic.

courage N. boldness, fearlessness, bravery, valor, heart.

course N. heading, direction, bearing.

court N. enclosure, quad, yard, atrium.

courtesy N. graciousness, respect, civility, politeness.

courtly ADJ. gracious, gallant, ceremonious.

cover V. hide, cap, conceal, shroud, mask.

covet V. envy, desire, want.

cowardly ADJ. timid, shy, afraid, weak.

crack V. split, break, snap, fissure.

cram V. crowd, stuff, fill, overfill.

cramp V. constrain.

crash N. collision, wreck, smash; —V. collide.

crave V. lust, desire, want, long for.

crawl V. creep, slide, worm.

craze N. fashion, enthusiasm, fad; —V. derange.

crazy ADJ. insane, enthusiastic, foolish, mad.

crease V. line, fold.

create V. make, produce, compose, invent, originate.

• **creative** ADJ. inventive, original. *She suggested an inventive ending for the play.*

credible ADJ. believable, authentic, conceivable.

credit N. belief, trust, faith, recognition, attribution; —V. believe, attribute.

creep V. sneak, crawl, steal, skulk, slip.

crime N. wrongdoing, offense, felony, violation, misdeed.

criminal ADJ. illegal, wrongful, unlawful; —N. crook, fugitive, outlaw, gangster.

cripple V. injure, maim, mutilate, disable.

• **crisis** N. emergency, juncture. *The citizens met the emergency with courage.*

critic N. reviewer, commentator, judge.

crooked ADJ. curved, winding, twisting, tortuous.

cross V. traverse, mix; —ADJ. annoyed, irritable, cranky.

crowd N. group, multitude, legion, assembly.

crown N. tiara, coronet, top, climax.

• **crucial** ADJ. decisive, critical, essential. *His decisive actions ensured victory.*

cruel ADJ. mean, pitiless, brutal, merciless.

crunch V. grind, chew.

crush V. smash, break, squeeze, mash.

cry V. sob, yell, shout, weep.

culminate V. end, climax, finish, result in, terminate.

cultivate V. grow, produce, develop, raise.

cultural ADJ. civilizing, refining, enlightening.

culture N. civilization, refinement, breeding, education.

cure V. remedy, heal; —N. medicine.

curiosity N. interest, inquisitiveness, prying, nosiness.

curse N. misfortune, evil, jinx, invective; —V. damn, accurse, swear.

curve V. bend, crook; —N. arch, arc, bow.

custom N. ritual, habit, practice, manner.

cut V. slice, chop, carve.

cutback N. decrease, reduction, curtailment.

cycle N. circle, process, circuit.

cynical ADJ. ironic, pessimistic, satirical, contemptuous, sardonic, sarcastic.

D

dainty ADJ. delicate, fine, petite, elegant.

damage N. harm, injury, breakage, destruction.

damn V. curse, condemn, swear.

damp ADJ. moist, humid, wet, dank, soggy.

dance V. step, foot it, gambol; —N. ball, party.

danger N. hazard, threat, peril, risk.

dangle V. hang, suspend, swing.

dare V. risk, brave, defy, challenge.

dark ADJ. dim, murky, obscure, black, somber.

darling ADJ. dear, favorite, beloved, precious.

dash V. rush, run, smash, break.

data N. evidence, information, statistics, facts.

dawn N. daybreak, sunrise, morning, birth.

daze V. confuse, stun, dazzle, blind.

dead ADJ. deceased, insensible, demised, lifeless, perished, departed, numb, exhausted.

deal N. transaction, agreement, affair; —V. barter, distribute, allocate.

dear ADJ. darling, favorite, beloved, expensive, costly.

death N. decease, demise, passing, fatality.

debase V. humble, dishonor, impair, corrupt, demean.

debate V. dispute, contend, argue.

debauch V. seduce, corrupt, defile, pervert.

debilitated ADJ. infirm, run-down.

debt N. arrears, liability, deficit, charge.

decadence N. deterioration, decay, retrogression.

decay V. deteriorate, decompose, go bad, spoil, rot.

deceit N. fraud, dishonesty, cunning, guile.

deceive V. mislead, fool, delude, beguile, cheat.

decent ADJ. correct, proper, clean, appropriate, acceptable.

deception N. treachery, deceit, subterfuge, ruse.

• **decide** V. conclude, determine, judge, resolve, settle. *We may conclude that the project is too expensive.*

declare V. say, proclaim, affirm, claim, announce, assert.

decline V. fade, deteriorate, decay, ebb.

decorate V. adorn, ornament, paint, enhance.

• **decrease** V. lessen, diminish, abate, decline. *Her absence will lessen our chances of success.*

deduction N. elimination, subtraction, discount; conclusion, judgment.

deep ADJ. bottomless, abysmal, profound, low.

defeat N. failure, beating, rebuff, destruction.

defect N. flaw, error, imperfection, fault, shortcoming.

defend V. guard, shield, protect, justify, vindicate.

defer V. delay, postpone, remit, adjourn.

deficient ADJ. lacking, incomplete, defective, flawed, insufficient.

• **definite** ADJ. certain, decided, clear-cut, precise, unambiguous, positive, certain, fixed, limited. *The time and date of the meeting are certain.*

defraud V. deceive, beguile, cheat, swindle.

defy V. oppose, dare, disobey, brave, challenge.

degrade V. demote, humble, debase.

degree N. proportion, rank, order, stage, grade, magnitude.

dejected ADJ. unhappy, depressed, discouraged, sad.

delay V. set back, detain, postpone, hesitate, slow; —N. deferment, suspension.

delete V. erase, drop, cancel, remove.

deliberate V. reason, ponder; —ADJ. intentional, planned, considered, unhurried, calculated, careful.

delicate ADJ. dainty, fragile, fine, weak, gentle.

delicious ADJ. delightful, palatable, tasty, pleasing, tasteful, toothsome, savory.

delight N. joy, enjoyment, pleasure; —V. enchant, please, gladden, cheer.

• **deliver** V. carry, convey, give, present. *Please carry our best wishes to your parents.*

delude V. deceive, fool, beguile, lead astray, corrupt.

• **demand** V. insist upon, ask for, request, require, involve, necessitate. *The customer should insist upon fair treatment.*

demeanor N. behavior, manner, attitude, bearing, air.

demise N. death, end, decease.

democratic ADJ. popular, self-governing, autonomous.

demonstration N. exhibition, presentation, display, show.

demote V. reduce, downgrade, lower.

demure ADJ. modest, coy, prudish, shy, bashful.

denial N. rejection, refusal, contradiction, negation.

denote V. designate, intend, imply, signify.

denunciate V. blame, accuse, condemn.

deny V. refuse, repudiate, contradict, reject.

depart V. go, leave, deviate.

• **depend** V. rely upon, expect, rest upon. *The adult children still rely upon their parents for support.*

depict V. represent, portray, describe, illustrate.

deplorable ADJ. shameful, disgraceful, regrettable, unfortunate.

deposit V. place, lay down, precipitate, put.

depreciate V. devalue, lower, belittle, cheapen, reduce.

depressed ADJ. melancholic, low, dejected, unhappy, sad, deprived, impoverished, underprivileged.

deprive V. rob, strip, bereave, deny.

depth N. profundity, drop, deepness.

derive V. obtain, get, acquire, take.

descend V. drop, fall, sink, deteriorate.

• **describe** V. explain, represent, relate, recount, communicate. *Please explain again how you redesigned the room.*

desert V. abandon, defect, quit, leave.

design V. draw, chart, plan, create; —N. project, plan, intention, idea.

designate V. indicate, specify, call, note.

desolate ADJ. empty, deserted, unhappy, miserable.

despair N. hopelessness, desperation, misery, despondence.

despise V. hate, condemn, dislike, scorn, distain.

destroy V. demolish, wreck, annihilate, break, kill.

destruct V. demolish, annihilate, wreck.

detach V. disengage, dismantle, separate, divide.

detail N. element, particular, item, circumstance; —V. itemize, tell, report.

detain V. hold, arrest, delay, keep, restrain.

detect V. perceive, discover, catch, expose, determine.

deter V. prevent, dissuade, stop, hinder, halt.

deteriorate V. erode, decay, degenerate, crumble, disintegrate, decline.

• **determine** V. judge, discover, ascertain, resolve, decide. *He will judge the success of our efforts.*

detest V. despise, hate, abominate, abhor.

detriment N. damage, injury, harm, disadvantage.

devastate V. waste, desolate, ravage, ruin, wreck.

• **develop** V. produce, generate, mature, elaborate, unfold, evolve. *The team must produce a workable plan soon.*

deviate V. swerve, diverge, err, depart.

devise V. make, plan, prepare, invent, design.

devotion N. adoration, sincerity, piety, observance, adherence.

dialect N. vernacular, argot, slang, accent, provincialism; standard speech, official language.

dictate V. impose, prescribe, decree, speak, tell.

dictator N. authoritarian, oppressor, tyrant, ruler.

die V. decease, perish, demise, expire, subside, fade.

differ V. vary, disagree, disaccord, dissent.

• **difference** N. inequality, variation, disparity, distinction, discrepancy. *We noted a grave inequality in economic opportunity.*

different ADJ. variant, unlike, perverse, dissimilar, distinctive.

diffident ADJ. shy, modest, timid, bashful.

digest V. assimilate, absorb, consume, eat; —N. summary, synopsis, précis.

dignify V. honor, exalt, elevate, grace.

dignity N. distinction, honor, elevation, nobility, elegance, eminence.

digress V. deviate, depart, diverge, stray, wander, err.

diligent ADJ. industrious, alert, studious, assiduous.

dilute ADJ. watered down, watery, weak, diluted; —V. thin, weaken, cut, reduce.

dim ADJ. shaded, obscure, dull, dark, unclear.

dip V. dunk, immerse, submerge, fall, drop.

dire ADJ. fateful, critical, dreadful, awful, grievous.

• **direct** V. guide, conduct, govern, supervise, control; —ADJ. immediate, frank, straightforward. *Please guide the guests to the nearest exit.*

dirty ADJ. soiled, foul, impure, unclean, filthy, polluted.

disable V. immobilize, cripple, paralyze, prostrate.

disappear V. evaporate, vanish, fade, depart, dissolve.

disappoint V. frustrate, discontent, let down, delude, foil.

disapprove V. object, refuse, disfavor, frown upon.

disaster N. catastrophe, accident, tragedy, misfortune, cataclysm.

disburse V. distribute, pay, expend.

discharge V. issue, unload, empty, emit, send out, demobilize, dismiss.

disciple N. follower, believer, student, pupil.

disclose V. expose, reveal, communicate, uncover, show.

discordant ADJ. incongruous, inharmonious, harsh, grating.

discourage V. depress, dishearten, dissuade.

• **discover** V. determine, find, reveal, ascertain, learn. *We wanted to determine how the pets escaped.*

discreet ADJ. cautious, delicate, conservative, prudent, wary, careful.

discrete ADJ. separate, individual.

• **discuss** V. consider, deliberate, talk over. *Next week the members will consider the proposal.*

disengage V. detach, break, undo, loosen, free.

disgrace N. shame, reproach, dishonor.

disgraceful ADJ. dishonorable, shameful, disreputable, ignominious, embarrassing.

disguise V. cover, cloak, mask; —N. costume, facade.

disgust N. repugnance, loathing, repulsion, aversion.

dishonest ADJ. false, deceitful, unfaithful, lying, corrupt.

disintegrate V. deteriorate, break up, ruin, destroy.

dismay N. terror, shock, fear, horror.

dismiss V. release, discharge, let go, eject, drop.

disobey V. defy, disregard, ignore, resist, rebel.

disorganized ADJ. disordered, messy, chaotic.

disparage V. belittle, lower, discredit.

disparity N. inequality, difference, gap.

dispel V. disperse, spread, scatter, dismiss.

disperse V. distribute, dispel, scatter, spread.

displace V. disturb, misplace, unseat, derange, disarrange.

display V. reveal, express, show, expose.

disposal N. elimination, discard, dumping, arrangement.

dispose V. arrange, incline, bias, adjust, settle, get rid of.

disposition N. character, sentiment, nature.

dissipate V. scatter, diffuse, spread, waste.

dissolve V. vanish, evaporate, melt destroy, fade.

dissonant ADJ. inharmonious, incongruous, harsh, grating.

distance N. remoteness, stretch, length, expanse; coldness, detachment.

distinct ADJ. separate, apparent, different, individual, diverse, various.

distinguish V. divide, separate, discriminate, characterize, differentiate, discern.

distort V. misrepresent, belie, pervert, deform.

distract V. occupy, amuse, divert, bewilder, derange, confuse.

distress N. worry, anguish, grievance, pain, agony, hurt, misery, anxiety.

- **distribute** V. hand out, dispense, deal, spread, arrange. *Two students will hand out fliers at the door.*

distrustful ADJ. dubious, suspicious, doubting, suspect, mistrustful.

disturb V. annoy, disrupt, disorder, agitate, displace, bother.

diverse ADJ. various, general, distinct, different.

divide V. separate, section, part, partition.

division N. partition, separation, section, piece, branch.

divorce V. divide, unmarry, split; —N. dissolution.

dizzy ADJ. dazzled, giddy, bewildered, light-headed, vertiginous, confused.

doctrine N. tenet, precept, principle, teaching, theory, belief, dogma.

dominant ADJ. controlling, prevailing, ruling, primary, commanding.

dominate V. control, prevail, command, rule, lead.

donation N. contribution, gift, benefaction, offering, charity.

doom N. fate, destiny; —V. condemn, sentence, ordain.

dote on V. adore, spoil, treasure.

double N. duplicate, copy, twin, counterpart; —ADJ. repeated, duplicated.

doubt N. concern, question, distrust, qualm, skepticism.

drag V. draw, pull, trail, tow.

drain V. exhaust, deplete, empty, tap.

dramatic ADJ. spectacular, theatrical, sensational.

draw V. picture, depict, sketch; attract, pull.

dread N. fear, anxiety, apprehension, terror, fright.

dream N. illusion, vision, reverie, ideal, aspiration.

dress V. clothe, attire, don; —N. clothing, clothes, garments, attire.

drink V. imbibe, swallow, guzzle, sip, absorb, ingest; —N. beverage, refreshment.

drive V. push, propel, shove, run, control, direct; —N. journey, ride, energy, effort, force.

droll ADJ. amusing, funny, humorous.

droop V. sink, slouch, wilt, sag.

drop V. descend, fall, omit, delete, eliminate; — N. drip, droplet, globule.

drug N. pharmaceutical, medicine, remedy, opiate, palliative.

drunk ADJ. inebriated, crapulous, loaded, besotted, high, tight.

dry ADJ. dehydrated, parched, arid, thirsty, dull, boring, bare.

dual ADJ. paired, binary, twofold.

dubious ADJ. doubtful, ambiguous, distrustful, unclear, suspicious, problematic.

duck V. evade, dip, avoid.

due ADJ. payable, owed, outstanding, unpaid, scheduled, anticipated, deserved.

dull ADJ. tiresome, boring, tedious, witless.

dumb ADJ. ignorant, dull, stupid, worthless, mute, speechless.

duplicate V. replicate, copy, reproduce, double; —N. facsimile.

• **duty** N. responsibility, purpose, function, job. *Each job involves an important responsibility.*

dwelling N. home, domicile, house, habitation.

E

eager ADJ. willing, anxious, ready, keen, impatient.

early ADJ. beginning, initial, primitive, ancient, untimely, premature; —ADV. ahead, beforehand, in advance.

earn V. merit, deserve, gain, collect.

earnest ADJ. determined, serious, grave, eager.

earth N. world, planet, globe, dirt, ground, soil.

ease N. comfort, tranquility, relaxation, facility, skillfulness.

- **easy** ADJ. simple, effortless, elementary, comfortable; —ADV. leisurely. *The kit came with simple instructions.*

eat V. devour, consume, bite, swallow.

ebb V. recede, subside, decrease.

eccentric ADJ. strange, idiosyncratic, unusual, odd, weird.

echo N. reverberation, repercussion; mimic, imitator; —V. reflect, rebound, repeat, imitate.

- **economical** ADJ. thrifty, prudent, frugal, wary. *His thrifty habits allowed him to save a great deal of money.*

ecstasy N. pleasure, delight, joy, bliss, rapture.

edge N. corner, rim, boundary, margin, brink, border.

edgy ADJ. nervous, anxious, excited, irritable.

edible ADJ. eatable, comestible.

- **educate** V. teach, instruct, inform, tutor, train.
  Few instructors could teach as well as he.

  effect N. result, consequence, impact, aftermath, outcome, influence, effectiveness, efficiency.

  effective ADJ. efficient, productive, practical, forceful.

  effeminate ADJ. feminine, womanly, delicate.

- **efficiency** N. capability, proficiency, effectiveness, practicality, pragmatism. *She had a down-to-earth sense of pragmatism about accomplishing her daily tasks.*

  effort N. struggle, exertion, endeavor, strain, striving.

  egocentric ADJ. egotistical, individualist, individualistic, selfish, self-centered.

  egotist N. narcissist, egoist.

  eject V. expel, banish, dismiss, jump, send out, bail out.

  elaborate ADJ. intricate, complicated, ornamented, decorated.

  elated ADJ. happy, joyful, overjoyed, ecstatic, euphoric, jubilant.

  elect V. vote, choose, select, ballot.

  elegant ADJ. cultivated, graceful, delicate, exquisite, refined.

  element N. component, part, factor, item, detail, point.

  elevate V. lift, boost, raise, heighten, amplify.

  eligible ADJ. suitable, worthy, qualified, fit.

- **eliminate** V. remove, omit, eradicate, excrete, purge. *The company goal was to remove all barriers to proper quality control.*

  eloquent ADJ. articulate, fluent, fecund, powerful, passionate, vocal.

  elude V. avoid, evade, escape, dodge, lose.

  embarrass V. perturb, confuse, faze, mortify, fluster.

  embody V. manifest, externalize, personify, typify, represent.

  embrace V. contain, accept, adopt, include, grasp, hug.

  embroil V. involve, complicate.

  emergency N. crisis, urgency, difficulty, predicament.

  eminent ADJ. prominent, celebrated, renowned, famous, distinguished.

  emit V. give, release, discharge, shed.

  emotion N. feeling, affection, sentiment.

- **emphasize** V. underline, stress, accentuate, point out. *He wanted to stress two important goals.*

- **employ** V. hire, use, apply, engage, retain. *She wanted to hire three day laborers.*

  empower V. authorize, enable, delegate, permit, license.

  empty ADJ. void, vacant, hollow, forsaken, abandoned, destitute.

  emulate V. follow, imitate.

- **enable** V. authorize, empower, allow, permit. *This document will authorize him to take action.*

enchant V. charm, captivate, enrapture, fascinate.

enclose V. surround, fence, cage.

encounter V. meet, face, confront; —N. confrontation, battle, clash.

encourage V. support, inspire, hearten, cheer, stimulate, promote.

endanger V. threaten, jeopardize, imperil, expose, risk.

endless ADJ. interminable, perpetual, continuous, eternal, infinite, ceaseless.

endurance N. strength, stamina, persistence, diligence, patience.

endure V. bear, tolerate, accept, withstand, continue, take.

energetic ADJ. dynamic, vigorous, determined, industrious, forceful.

enforce V. implement, invoke, execute, effect.

engage V. occupy, involve, attract, commission, hire, employ.

enhance V. promote, intensify, improve, flatter.

enjoy V. savor, appreciate, relish, admire.

• **enlighten** V. inform, illume, illuminate, educate, teach. *The book can inform you about space travel.*

enormous ADJ. huge, giant, gigantic, outrageous, colossal, immense.

enrage V. anger, madden, infuriate, incense, provoke, exasperate.

enter V. start, join, penetrate, intrude, post.

enterprise N. venture, undertaking, project, company, business.

entertain V. amuse, capture, interest, divert.

enthusiasm N. passion, zeal, eagerness, fervor.

entice V. tempt, attract, charm, allure, draw.

entirely ADV. completely, wholly, solely.

entry N. entrance, admission, insertion.

enumerate V. number, itemize, count, list.

enunciate V. state, pronounce.

envelop V. wrap, surround, blanket, enclose, cover.

• **environment** N. habitat, surrounding conditions, vicinity, climate, atmosphere. *The mice seemed to enjoy their new habitat.*

envy N. jealousy, covetousness, enviousness.

epitomize V. review, capture, represent.

• **equal** ADJ. same, equivalent, even, identical. *The parents wanted to give both children the same advantages.*

equitable ADJ. fair, equal, honest, impartial, just.

equivocal ADJ. ambiguous, uncertain, indefinite, doubtful, enigmatic.

eradicate V. exterminate, abolish, destroy, decimate, nullify, annihilate.

erase V. obliterate, cancel, annihilate, remove.

erotic ADJ. passionate, sexual, sensual, fervent, carnal, amorous, lustful, concupiscent.

erudite ADJ. sage, wise, learned, well-educated.

escalate V. increase, magnify.

escape V. elude, run away, flee, avoid.

escort V. guide, protect, accompany, guard; —N. companion.

essay N. test, composition, paper, thesis, dissertation, article.

essence N. substance, base, quintessence, heart.

• **essential** ADJ. fundamental, vital, elemental, intrinsic, necessary, integral. *I think the speaker neglected one fundamental point.*

• **establish** V. found, institute, base, install, settle, prove. *Next week they will have found a nonprofit charitable organization.*

esteem N. admiration, respect, regard, appreciation, honor.

estimate V. assess, appraise, value, approximate, rate.

eternal ADJ. endless, perpetual, everlasting.

eternity N. infinity, forever, endlessness, immortality.

ethical ADJ. good, honest, right, virtuous, moral, proper, decent, righteous.

evade V. avoid, dodge, lose, escape.

evaporate V. disappear, vanish, vaporize.

evasive ADJ. equivocal, shifty, elusive, dishonest.

even ADJ. flat, level, smooth, straight, flush, equal, uniform, regular, constant.

everyday ADJ. mundane, common, commonplace, routine.

- **evident** ADJ. apparent, plain, obvious, discernible, visible. *The truth was apparent to all of us.*

  evil N. nefarious, black, sinful, wrong.

  evoke V. excite, elicit, summon, educe, draw.

  evolve V. develop, emerge, grow, elaborate.

  exact ADJ. precise, accurate, close, strict, correct, faultless.

  exaggerate V. magnify, inflate, overstate, stretch.

  exalt V. honor, praise, elevate, glorify.

  examine V. analyze, check, inspect, study, view.

- **example** N. illustration, prototype, symbol, instance. *Perhaps this illustration will help make my point.*

  exceed V. surpass, overrun, overreach, excel, eclipse.

- **excellent** ADJ. superior, marvelous, splendid, great, terrific, first, fine, wonderful. *The crew was made up of superior athletes.*

- **exceptional** ADJ. rare, outstanding, different, unusual. *The guests brought a rare bottle of wine to the dinner party.*

  excess N. abundance, plethora, overabundance, surplus; —ADJ. profuse.

  excessive ADJ. extreme, overabundant, undue, exorbitant, extravagant, immoderate.

  exchange V. change, interchange, trade, swap.

  excite V. arouse, provoke, inspire, stimulate.

  exclaim V. cry, blurt, shout, call.

excuse N. reason, apology, explanation; —V. forgive, justify, absolve, relieve.

execute V. perform, fulfill, enforce, effect, administer.

exercise N. activity, play, sport, practice, training.

exertion N. endeavor, effort, attempt, exercise.

exhaust V. fatigue, tire, deplete, wear out, consume, finish.

exhibit V. display, show, demonstrate.

exist V. live, consist, be, subsist.

existing ADJ. present, alive, living, actual.

expand V. increase, spread, elaborate, amplify, widen.

expect V. envision, hope, await, anticipate.

• **expectation** N. anticipation, prospect. *In anticipation of his visit, the town leaders prepared a parade and banquet.*

expedite V. speed up, hasten, rush, facilitate, accelerate.

expel V. eject, banish, remove, evict, oust.

expend V. spend, use, consume, exhaust.

experience V. feel, undergo, go through, live, encounter; —N. knowledge, training, event, occurrence.

expert N. authority, master, specialist, professional.

• **explain** V. clarify, explicate, resolve, account for, interpret. *Please clarify the technical terms used in the manual.*

explanation N. definition, description, clarification, interpretation, account.

explode V. blow up, detonate, burst, blow.

exploit V. use, manipulate, abuse.

• **explore** V. investigate, inquire, examine, delve. *The researchers want to investigate the topic more thoroughly.*

expose V. display, reveal, uncover, disclose.

• **express** V. convey, communicate, declare, state. *Please convey our gratitude to Mr. Evans.*

extend V. expand, widen, increase, spread, lengthen.

extent N. stretch, length, degree, size.

exterminate V. eradicate, kill, annihilate, destroy, rid, decimate.

extinguish V. abolish, destroy, quench, douse, suppress.

extra ADJ. additional, superfluous, another.

extravagant ADJ. lavish, excessive, profuse, wasteful.

• **extreme** ADJ. utmost, furthermost, farthest, uttermost, greatest. *We devoted the utmost effort to the project.*

exuberant ADJ. buoyant, vivacious, high-spirited, effervescent, profuse.

eye V. look, detect, discern, watch, gaze.

F

fabricate V. make, produce, manufacture, invent; fake, counterfeit, feign.

face V. encounter, confront, meet, challenge.

facile ADJ. easy, dexterous, ready, flexible, clever.

facility N. ease, ability, fluency, skillfulness.

- **fact** N. certainty, truth, actuality, circumstance. *His retirement is a certainty, not supposition.*

- **factor** N. element, circumstance, part. *We counted on the element of surprise in announcing our plans.*

faculty N. capacity, competence, talent, ability.

fade V. decline, deteriorate, dissolve, disappear.

fail V. collapse, break, falter, omit, fade.

failure N. unsuccessfulness, neglect, default, shortage, deterioration.

faint ADJ. weak, muffled, inaudible, feeble, low, unclear; —V. pass out.

fair ADJ. impartial, unprejudiced, objective; light, blond; average, ordinary.

faith N. belief, creed, religion, persuasion.

faithful ADJ. devoted, loyal, allegiant, resolute, authentic, accurate.

fake V. counterfeit, simulate, pretend, feign, falsify, fabricate.

fall V. collapse, decline, drop, topple, plunge.

fallacious ADJ. false, irrational, invalid, delusive, deceptive, erroneous.

fallacy N. error, untruth, falsehood.

• **false** ADJ. fallacious, delusive, deceptive, erroneous, untrue, dishonest. *They were accused of spreading fallacious rumors.*

falsify V. fake, distort, lie, misstate, misrepresent.

familiar ADJ. conscious, aware, acquainted, informed; friendly, intimate, common.

family N. house, kindred, household, ancestry, lineage, loved ones.

• **famous** ADJ. eminent, popular, notorious, famed. *The eminent lawyer rose to speak.*

fan N. enthusiast, follower, devotee.

fanatic N. extremist, enthusiast, devotee.

fancy N. notion, taste, humor; —ADJ. elaborate, ornate, deluxe, exclusive.

fantastic ADJ. incredible, fabulous, imaginary, unimaginable, unbelievable.

fare V. manage, go, eat; —N. ticket price.

fascinate V. charm, attract, enthrall.

fashion N. style, mode, vogue, craze; —V. make, adapt, mold, shape.

fast ADJ. speedy, quick, rapid, swift; —ADV. quickly.

fasten V. tie, fix, attach, bind, connect.

fat ADJ. obese, overweight, portly, corpulent, stout, weighty.

fatal ADJ. catastrophic, deadly, fateful, destructive.

fate N. predestination, destiny, luck, chance, fortune.

fatigue N. exhaustion, weakness, weariness.

favor N. service, kindness, indulgence, courteousness; —V. esteem, prefer.

• **favorite** ADJ. preferred, favored, popular, liked; —N. darling. *Her preferred sport was tennis.*

fear N. dread, panic, alarm, trepidation, anxiety, fright.

fearful ADJ. alarming, dreadful, frightening, ghastly, terrible; anxious, nervous.

feast N. meal, banquet, festival.

feat N. trick, act, deed, performance, accomplishment.

feeble ADJ. tenuous, weak, frail.

• **feel** V. sense, know, experience, savor, touch, taste, perceive. *I sense that you are feeling uncomfortable.*

feeling N. sentiment, sensation, belief, intuition, impression, idea.

feminine ADJ. femaleness, effeminacy, maidenly, womanly, delicate, tender.

fertile ADJ. productive, prolific, fruitful, rich, abundant.

fervent ADJ. passionate, earnest, enthusiastic, ardent, vehement.

feverish ADJ. hot, fervid, overheated.

fiction N. story, tale, fantasy, myth, dream.

fierce ADJ. violent, savage, ferocious, vicious, cruel.

fiery ADJ. spirited, hot, passionate, fervid, blazing.

fight V. dispute, clash, battle, contend, struggle.

figure N. design, form, shape, pattern, outline.

fill V. pack, load, pile, satisfy, feed, charge, pervade.

filthy ADJ. rotten, foul, dirty, obscene, disgusting, abhorrent, squalid, vile.

finance V. fund, subsidize, bank, back, capitalize.

find V. locate, discover, spot, detect, pinpoint.

fine ADJ. superior, excellent, delicate, subtle, thin.

finish V. conclude, end, terminate, complete, close; —N. conclusion, completion, termination.

fire N. flame, blaze; passion, enthusiasm, radiance, brilliance.

firm ADJ. solid, hard, strong, resolute, determined, sound, decisive, settled, flat, fixed.

first ADJ. primary, original, earliest, initial.

fit ADJ. appropriate, suitable, proper, prepared, ready; —V. suit, match, adapt, become.

fitting ADJ. proper, just, appropriate, suitable.

fix V. fasten, tie, attach, mend, repair, adjust, pinpoint, decide, establish.

flagrant ADJ. glaring, arrant, conspicuous, bold, outrageous.

flash V. shimmer, sparkle, gleam, blink, display.

flat ADJ. horizontal, recumbent, even, level, dull, tasteless, flavorless.

flattery N. compliment, adulation, praise, blandishment.

flavor N. savor, taste, essence, atmosphere, aroma, quality.

• **flexible** ADJ. pliant, elastic, limber, bending, lithe. *A pliant sheet of plastic covered the opening.*

flirt V. toy, dally, coquet, trifle, toy with, play with, tease.

flood N. deluge, torrent, inundation, overflow, cataclysm.

flourish V. thrive, bloom, prosper, grow, increase.

flow V. run, circulate, stream, pour, course.

flush ADJ. flat, even, level; —N. blush; —V. empty, purge.

flutter V. hover, flicker, shake, tremble, oscillate.

fly V. wing, sail, flap, dart, shoot, run, escape.

focus N. center, concentration, centrum, emphasis.

• **follow** V. chase, pursue, imitate, ensue, heed, observe. *The dogs refused to chase the fox.*

fond ADJ. affectionate, dear, tender, loving.

food N. sustenance, nourishment, aliment, bread, edibles, comestibles, foodstuff.

fool N. imbecile, idiot, ass, moron, simpleton; — V. trick, deceive, delude, beguile.

forbid V. ban, interdict, restrain, exclude, disallow.

forbidden ADJ. prohibited, banned, impermissible.

force N. vitality, power, vigor, muscle, energy; — V. pressure, compel, coerce.

foreign ADJ. strange, exotic, alien, external.

foretell V. prophesy, predict, divine.

forget V. overlook, disregard, omit, neglect.

forgive V. excuse, remit, pardon, condone, absolve.

form N. shape, pattern, figure, format, cast; —V. mold, develop, shape, cast, pattern, constitute.

formal ADJ. ceremonious, ritualistic, orderly, methodical.

formulate V. invent, devise, frame, draft, concoct.

fortify V. bolster, gird, strengthen, confirm.

fortune N. fate, luck, chance, destiny; riches, wealth.

forward V. send, advance onward; —ADJ. foremost, first, ahead, leading; arrogant, bold, impudent.

fragile ADJ. brittle, delicate, breakable, weak.

fragrance N. perfume, scent, aroma, bouquet.

frail ADJ. fragile, delicate, infirm.

frank ADJ. direct, straightforward, open, honest, candid.

frantic ADJ. frenzied, wild, delirious, mad, hysterical.

free ADJ. independent, liberated, unrestrained, gratuitous; —V. release, liberate, emancipate.

freedom N. independence, liberty, sovereignty.

- **frequent** ADJ. recurrent, repeated, continual, many, common. *The child had recurrent nightmares.*

  frequently ADV. usually, regularly, repeatedly, generally.

  fresh ADJ. new, current, novel, healthy, green, different, recent.

  friend N. acquaintance, companion, comrade, colleague, pal.

  frighten V. intimidate, scare, terrify, terrorize, startle, alarm.

  frigid ADJ. cold, bitter, freezing, glacial, icy; passionless, unresponsive.

  front N. facade, face, head, beginning, start.

  frown V. scowl, glare, sulk, disapprove.

  frustrate V. defeat, baffle, disappoint, hinder, halt.

- **fulfill** V. satisfy, execute, perform, complete, accomplish. *He decided to satisfy a longtime goal.*

  fumble V. botch, drop, muddle, grope, mess up.

  fun N. play, amusement, gaiety, enjoyment, entertainment.

- **function** N. role, purpose, use, celebration, ceremony, gathering; —v. work, operate, act, run, behave. *Your role in the company will be crucial.*

- **fundamental** ADJ. essential, elemental, basic, principal, primary. *You have overlooked an essential fact.*

  furious ADJ. raging, enraged, inflamed, angry, mad, infuriated, ranting.

furnish V. provide, give, equip, supply.

futile ADJ. ineffective, unsuccessful, useless, fruitless.

• **future** ADJ. impending, approaching, coming, imminent. *We cannot ignore impending pressures.*

fuzzy ADJ. blurred, obscure, unclear, out of focus, indistinct.

G

gadget N. contrivance, contraption, concern, gizmo, doodad.

gain V. acquire, get, recover, earn.

gallant ADJ. chivalrous, gracious, brave, valiant, courageous.

gamble V. wager, bet, venture, speculate, stake.

game N. sport, pastime, amusement, recreation, fun.

gang N. mob, pack, band, group, crew.

gap N. break, breach, interim, chasm, opening.

garish ADJ. gaudy, showy, ostentatious, flashy, vulgar.

garment N. dress, clothes, attire, garb.

gasp V. pant, wheeze, heave.

gather V. collect, accumulate, assemble, group, harvest.

gaudy ADJ. loud, showy, bold, tacky, tasteless, cheap.

gauge N. thickness, diameter, standard; —V. measure, evaluate, size, estimate.

gaunt ADJ. haggard, emaciated, wasted, thin.

gay ADJ. happy, jovial, merry, gleeful; —N. homosexual.

• **general** ADJ. common, universal, expansive, widespread, diverse, comprehensive. *We acted for the common good.*

- **generate** V. produce, develop, engender, cause.
  The staff members produce dozens of letters each day.

generosity N. magnanimity, openhandedness, liberality.

generous ADJ. unselfish, charitable, liberal, free, openhearted, magnanimous.

genesis N. birth, beginning, creation, start.

genial ADJ. pleasing, gracious, kind, pleasant, amiable.

genteel ADJ. prim, polite, proper, polished, cultured, kind.

gentle ADJ. tender, soft, kind, mild, calm, soothing.

genuine ADJ. reliable, sincere, honest, authentic, real.

germ N. microbe, bug, embryo, kernel, seed.

gesture N. sign, expression, signal, indication, motion.

get V. obtain, acquire, procure, receive, earn, attain, secure.

ghastly ADJ. awful, terrible, shocking, hideous, horrid.

ghost N. shadow, specter, spirit, apparition, phantom.

giant N. mammoth, behemoth; —ADJ. immense, massive, huge, enormous, monumental.

giddy ADJ. lighthearted, frivolous, flighty, silly.

gift N. donation, present, gratuity, talent, aptitude.

giggle V. laugh, snicker, titter.

gimmick N. contrivance, gadget, trick, wrinkle.

gird V. secure, fortify, support, bind.

give V. present, furnish, supply, donate, impart, grant.

glad ADJ. pleased, delighted, happy, gay, joyous, cheerful.

glance V. glimpse, sight, view, look, appear.

glare N. blaze, blare, glower, scowl, frown.

gleam V. shine, sparkle, glitter, flash.

glean V. garner, extract, cull, collect, harvest.

glib ADJ. articulate, fluent, vocal, suave, glossy.

glide V. flow, slip, slick, lapse.

glitter V. glisten, flash, sparkle, shimmer.

gloom N. dejection, depression, melancholy, sadness, unhappiness, blues.

gloomy ADJ. melancholy, sad, depressed, depressing, dark, dreary, dismal.

glorious ADJ. splendorous, sublime, magnificent, majestic, superb, beautiful.

glum ADJ. gloomy, morose, sullen, sour, sad, dismal.

go V. depart, leave, proceed, run, walk, travel, stride.

go-between N. intermediary, mediator, broker, middleman.

• **good** ADJ. pleasing, flawless, perfect, sound, whole, pleasant. *The pleasing sounds of violins drifted through the restaurant.*

gossip N. murmur, hearsay, whispering, stories.

govern V. manage, control, command, administer, rule, lead.

government N. administration, rule, direction, control.

grab V. seize, grasp, catch, grip.

grace N. elegance, ease, gracefulness, beauty, charm.

graceful ADJ. elegant, beautiful, smooth, harmonious, stylish, nimble, dexterous.

grade N. rank, level, stage; ascent; quality, class.

gradual ADJ. continuous, slow, step-by-step, moderate, gentle.

grand ADJ. magnificent, majestic, splendid, sublime, superb, great.

grant N. allowance, gift, allocation, contribution; —V. concede, permit, yield, allow.

graphic ADJ. realistic, lifelike, vivid, photographic, illustrative, written.

grasp V. clutch, seize, grip, clasp, grab, take.

grateful ADJ. thankful, appreciative, gratified, pleasant.

gratifying ADJ. enjoyable, satisfying, pleasant, agreeable.

gratuity N. tip, contribution, donation, offering.

grave ADJ. serious, severe, momentous, solemn, earnest.

great ADJ. huge, majestic, large, big, gigantic, excellent, splendid, super.

greed N. covetousness, avarice, cupidity, avidity.

greedy ADJ. avid, covetous, hungry, rapacious, stingy.

greet V. welcome, salute, hail, receive.

grief N. sorrow, heartbreak, woe, sadness, mourning.

grieve V. mourn, suffer, bemoan, lament, weep, sadden.

grind V. crush, pulverize, sharpen, smooth.

grip V. grasp, seize, hold, clutch.

gross ADJ. rough, obscene, vulgar; thick, enormous, fat, bulky.

ground N. property, land, surface, earth, soil.

group N. bunch, collection, assembly, gathering, set; —V. collect, gather, classify.

grow V. increase, enlarge, develop, produce, raise, cultivate.

gruff ADJ. coarse, abrupt, rude, blunt.

grumble V. mutter, complain, fuss, protest.

guarantee V. attest, verify, certify, testify, assure; —N. warranty, assurance, promise, oath, pledge.

guard V. protect, watch, guide, keep, secure.

guardian N. custodian, keeper, warden, protector, trustee.

• **guess** V. suppose, presume, infer, suspect, assume. *I suppose two cakes will be enough for the party.*

guide V. lead, direct, show, escort, conduct; —N. conductor, escort, leader.

guilty ADJ. corrupt, criminal, immoral.

H

habit N. custom, inclination, tendency, practice.

habitual ADJ. accustomed, customary, routine, usual.

haggard ADJ. worn, gaunt, fatigued, tired, exhausted.

haggle V. bargain, deal, barter, trade, squabble.

hail V. welcome, greet, honor, address.

hairy ADJ. furry, woolly, fleecy.

hallow V. sanctify, devote.

hallowed ADJ. sacred, holy, sanctified, consecrated, revered.

hallucination N. illusion, fantasy, delusion.

halt V. stop, falter, stand, arrest, hesitate.

hamper V. prevent, obstruct, thwart, hinder.

hand N. assistant, helper, aid, support; —V. pass, give, bequeath.

handicap N. disadvantage, advantage (in sports), hindrance, limitation.

handy ADJ. useful, helpful, convenient, skilled, clever, inventive, resourceful.

hang V. attach, suspend, swing, execute, lynch.

happiness N. joy, gladness, cheerfulness, bliss, contentment, rapture, peace.

- **happy** ADJ. joyous, glad, gay, cheerful, pleased, merry, fulfilled. *Congratulations on this joyous occasion.*

harass V. annoy, irritate, besiege, tantalize, taunt, incense.

harbor N. port, anchorage; —V. protect, shelter, shield, cover.

hard ADJ. tough, rugged, firm, strong, solid, severe, difficult, burdensome.

harden V. toughen, solidify, petrify; confirm.

harm N. hurt, injury, damage, detriment.

harmless ADJ. innocuous, innocent, benign, inoffensive, gentle, good.

harmonious ADJ. agreeable, concordant, congruous, amicable, melodious.

harmony N. consonance, accord, unity, agreement, kinship, peace, affinity.

harsh ADJ. grating, discordant, rough, bleak, bitter.

harvest N. gathering, reaping, crop, yield; —V. reap, gather.

haste N. speed, hurry, rapidity, rush.

hasty ADJ. quick, abrupt, hurried.

hatch V. originate, plot, invent, produce.

hate V. despise, detest, abhor, loathe, resent, disapprove.

have V. possess, own, hold, retain, contain.

haze N. fog, mist, film, smoke, murk.

head N. commander, director, supervisor, boss; —V. administer, direct, lead; —ADJ. chief, foremost, top.

health N. healthiness, soundness, wholeness, heartiness.

healthy ADJ. robust, sound, strong, hearty, flourishing.

heap N. pile, mass, bunch, pyramid; —V. pile, mound, lump, load, shower.

hear V. detect, listen, perceive.

heart N. core, essence, center, breast, bosom, sentiment, sympathy.

heat N. hotness, warmth, excitement, fervor.

heave V. throw, toss, boost, pull.

heaven N. paradise, rapture, ecstasy, delight, bliss, happiness.

heaviness N. weight, gravity, ponderosity, heftiness.

heavy ADJ. weighty, massive, hefty, burdensome, cumbersome.

hedge V. surround, equivocate, skirt, brush.

heedful ADJ. attentive, mindful, careful.

heedless ADJ. inattentive, careless, unmindful, deaf.

hefty ADJ. severe, heavy, strong, tough.

heighten V. intensify, increase, concentrate, elevate.

• **help** V. support, aid, assist, bolster. *Your support has meant so much to us all.*

• **helpful** ADJ. useful, supportive, assistive, effective, constructive, beneficial, practical. *Criticism is welcomed so long as it is useful.*

• **helpless** ADJ. powerless, feeble, dependent, weak, unprotected. *The company was powerless to prevent the takeover.*

heritage N. birthright, legacy, inheritance, tradition.

hero N. celebrity, champion, idol.

• **hesitate** V. pause, waver, falter, delay. *Usually she will pause before stepping on stage.*

hidden ADJ. secluded, blind, ulterior.

hide V. cover, obscure, conceal, disguise, protect, veil.

high ADJ. elevated, towering, tall, shrill, strong, heavy.

higher ADJ. superior, greater, senior, over, above.

hill N. projection, rise, hillock, mound, eminence, prominence.

• **hinder** V. prevent, impede, obstruct, hold back. *Your physical condition may prevent you from participating.*

hint N. suggestion, clue, indication, allusion; —V. allude, imply, suggest.

hire V. employ, lease, rent, engage.

history N. chronicle, story, account, past, record, archives.

hit V. strike, punch, discover, find, slap.

hitch V. harness, tie, fasten; —N. hindrance, catch, obstacle.

hoard N. store, reservoir, inventory, stockpile; — V. amass, store, stock, gather.

hoarse ADJ. harsh, rough, grating, husky.

hold V. retain, keep, embrace, grasp, believe, think.

hole N. orifice, opening, cavity, aperture, den, burrow, cave.

hollow ADJ. concave, empty, vacant, cavernous.

holy ADJ. sacred, pious, religious, divine, blessed, devout.

homage N. honor, respect, reverence, tribute, devotion.

home N. dwelling, residence, house, lodging, habitat, refuge, sanctuary, asylum.

• **honest** ADJ. truthful, sincere, just, trustworthy, honorable, righteous, frank. *His truthful testimony influenced the grand jury.*

• **honesty** N. straightforwardness, integrity, honor, rectitude, fairness. *Our response will depend upon your straightforwardness in this matter.*

honor N. esteem, respect, deference, homage, reputation.

• **hope** V. aspire, desire; —N. expectation, belief, trust. *The two students aspire to become famous ballerinas.*

• **hopeful** ADJ. optimistic, aspirant, confident; —N. aspirant. *Their optimistic attitudes help them succeed.*

hopeless ADJ. impossible, incurable, useless, futile, desperate.

horrible ADJ. ghastly, terrible, awful, dreadful.

horror N. dread, terror, fear, abhorrence.

• **hostile** ADJ. unfriendly, contentious, inimical, argumentative. *Unfriendly forces surrounded the platoon.*

hostility N. belligerence, aggression, antipathy, antagonism.

hot ADJ. burning, scalding, torrid, flaming, blazing, passionate.

house N. residence, home, dwelling.

hover V. hang, linger, flutter, fly.

howl V. yell, wail, cry, scream.

hue N. tone, color, shade, tint.

• **huge** ADJ. enormous, large, big, gigantic, immense. *An enormous fossil was discovered in Montana.*

hum V. whir, buzz, drone.

human N. mortal, man, person, creature, Homo sapiens.

humanitarian ADJ. compassionate, benevolent, merciful, humane.

humble ADJ. meek, docile, mild, modest, unassuming.

humiliate V. demean, disgrace, humble.

humor N. comedy, joking, amusement, wit, disposition, mood, sentiment; —V. placate, indulge, oblige, gratify.

humorous ADJ. funny, witty, amusing, comical.

hunch N. suspicion, feeling, premonition, intuition.

hunger N. desire, appetite.

hungry ADJ. starved, avid, famished, ravenous.

hunt V. pursue, chase, stalk, drive, search, probe, seek.

hurt V. wound, damage, injure, harm.

hush V. silence, quiet, repress, cover.

hustle V. hasten, rush, run, dash, hurry.

hyperbole N. exaggeration, overstatement.

hypnotic ADJ. irresistible, mesmerizing, sleepy, quieting, lethargic.

hypocrisy N. insincerity, delusion, falsehood, cant, sham.

hypocritical ADJ. insincere, dishonest, two-faced, deceptive, sanctimonious, dishonorable.

hypothesis N. theory, conjecture, speculation, supposition, postulate.

hypothetical ADJ. theoretical, speculative, imaginary, conjectural, symbolic.

I

icy ADJ. frigid, frozen, cold, frosty.

- **idea** N. concept, image, belief, opinion, meaning, significance. *Your concept for a new engine interests us.*

  ideal N. model, vision, dream; —ADJ. perfect, visionary, illusory, excellent, complete.

  identical ADJ. equal, uniform, equivalent, same.

  identify V. distinguish, recognize, characterize, sympathize, point out.

  identity N. personality, individuality, character, self.

  idiot N. fool, moron, dope.

  idle ADJ. inactive, lazy, slothful, unemployed, unused.

  ignite V. spark, inflame, light, detonate.

  ignorance N. illiteracy, innocence, unmindfulness.

- **ignorant** ADJ. illiterate, uneducated, stupid, unlearned, unlettered, shallow. *The illiterate man could not read the warning signs.*

  ignore V. neglect, disregard, overlook, slight.

  ill ADJ. sick, diseased, evil, bad, unhealthy.

  ill-considered ADJ. unwise, precipitate.

  illegal ADJ. lawless, wrongful, unauthorized, forbidden, prohibited.

  illegitimate ADJ. unlawful, illicit, illegal, improper, unlicensed, fatherless, bastard.

illicit ADJ. unlawful, illegal, criminal, unethical.

illiterate ADJ. ignorant, unlettered, uneducated, unlearned.

illness N. sickness, disease, malady.

illogical ADJ. unreasonable, superfluous, absurd, unsettled, inconclusive.

ill-tempered ADJ. irritable, bad-tempered, grouchy, crabby, petulant.

illuminate V. enlighten, illume, light up, clarify, explain, light.

illusive ADJ. delusive, illusory, hallucinatory.

illustrate V. portray, express, depict, clarify.

image N. representation, likeness, double, idea, appearance.

• **imagination** N. conception, thought, fancy, fantasy, creativity. *His primary value to the company was his power of conception.*

imagine V. envision, conceive, picture, visualize, fantasize.

imbibe V. drink, absorb, sip.

imitate V. mimic, parody, mock, echo, copy.

immature ADJ. young, precocious, childish.

• **immediate** ADJ. instantaneous, direct, primary, close, prompt. *An instantaneous temperature drop followed the storm.*

• **immense** ADJ. huge, enormous, gigantic, large. *Huge piles of grain awaited processing.*

immoral ADJ. evil, wrong, impure, lecherous, indecent, unprincipled.

immortal ADJ. endless, undying, eternal, perpetual, everlasting.

immovable ADJ. fixed, anchored, stable, rooted, immobile.

impact N. collision, force, clash, percussion, shock.

impartial ADJ. neutral, fair, nonpartisan, unprejudiced.

impatient ADJ. nervous, anxious, fretful, eager, restless.

impeccable ADJ. perfect, flawless, spotless, immaculate, faultless.

impede V. hinder, halt, stop, prevent, hamper, delay, block.

imperative ADJ. essential, unavoidable, critical, required, urgent.

imperceptible ADJ. invisible, negligible, slight, subtle, insignificant.

imperfect ADJ. defective, faulty, blemished, inadequate.

impersonate V. portray, pose, imitate, act, represent.

impertinent ADJ. trivial, irrelevant, impudent, inapplicable.

impetuous ADJ. impulsive, precipitate, rash, hasty, reckless.

implausible ADJ. unbelievable, suspect, inconceivable, doubtful, questionable.

implement V. use, enforce, achieve; —N. instrument, device, tool.

implicit ADJ. understood, unsaid, implied, tacit.

imply V. hint, indicate, suggest.

import N. substance, purport, amount, meaning, importance, significance.

• **importance** N. significance, import, weight, consequence, concern. *They misunderstood the significance of the discovery.*

• **important** ADJ. consequential, meaningful, influential, significant, substantial, weighty. *Two weeks of deliberation were required to consider the consequential matter.*

impose V. demand, inflict, require.

• **impossible** ADJ. infeasible, unworkable, impractical. *Your reforms may prove infeasible.*

impotent ADJ. helpless, powerless, weak, frail, harmless.

impractical ADJ. impossible, unworkable, infeasible, unattainable, unachievable, unrealistic.

impress V. engrave, pound, drive, excite, arrest, stir, move.

• **impression** N. interpretation, understanding, mark, feeling, effect, influence; indentation, print. *Please tell us your interpretation of the play.*

improper ADJ. inappropriate, unfit, unseemingly, unsuitable.

• **improve** V. refine, amend, better, upgrade, repair, help. *We plan to refine the process before beginning production.*

impudent ADJ. brazen, presumptuous, smart, audacious, arrogant, rude, disrespectful.

impulsive ADJ. spontaneous, rash, hasty, impatient, fiery.

impure ADJ. unclean, defiled, corrupt, mixed, alloyed, crude.

inaccessible ADJ. unreachable, inconvenient, unattainable.

inaccurate ADJ. wrong, incorrect, erroneous, false.

inactive ADJ. still, idle, inoperative, motionless.

• **inadequate** ADJ. insufficient, incompetent, unqualified, incapable. *The agency has insufficient resources.*

incalculable ADJ. measureless, infinite, countless, limitless, enormous.

incident N. evident, happening, occurrence, circumstance.

incisive ADJ. shrewd, perceptive, discerning, acute, penetrating.

incline V. lean, tend, slope, tilt, list.

incompetent ADJ. inefficient, unqualified, unfit, incapable, unskilled, irresponsible.

incomprehensible ADJ. unintelligible, impenetrable, unfathomable, incompetent.

incongruous ADJ. incompatible, inconsistent, conflicting, foreign, dissonant.

inconsistent ADJ. conflicting, incongruous, fluctuating, capricious, unsteady, incompatible.

inconspicuous ADJ. unobtrusive, obscure, unnoticed, retiring.

inconvenience N. trouble, discomfort.

incorrect ADJ. false, wrong, erroneous, inaccurate.

• **increase** V. enlarge, amplify, expand, rise, augment, swell; —N. boost, enlargement, addition, augmentation. *They can enlarge the seating area by adding temporary bleachers.*

incredible ADJ. astonishing, fantastic, fabulous, unbelievable, impossible.

indecent ADJ. obscene, offensive, improper, shocking.

indefinite ADJ. undetermined, general, indistinct, vague, unclear, obscure.

indelicate ADJ. tactless, improper, unbecoming, offensive.

independence N. separation, freedom, sovereignty, self-reliance, autonomy, self-sufficience.

• **indicate** V. designate, show, mark, testify, attest. *You should designate a second driver.*

indifference N. apathy, insensitivity, insignificance, unimportance.

indifferent ADJ. detached, nonchalant, cool, insensitive.

indigenous ADJ. native, existing, innate, natural, inherent.

indignity N. insult, outrage, offense, disrespect, humiliation.

indisposed ADJ. unwilling, reluctant, disinclined, sickly.

- **individual** ADJ. particular, singular, separate, different, unique, personal. *No one else has her particular skills.*

  indoctrinate V. instruct, teach, initiate, instill, propagandize.

  indulge V. participate, satisfy, concede, cherish, please, humor.

  industry N. business, enterprise, diligence, persistence.

  ineffectiveness N. ineffectuality, futility.

- **inefficient** ADJ. wasteful, unproductive, inept, incompetent, unskilled. *The whole city practiced wasteful habits for garbage disposal.*

  inept ADJ. unskilled, inefficient, awkward, clumsy, unhandy.

  inequality N. disproportion, disparity, irregularity.

  inexcusable ADJ. unjustifiable, unforgivable, unpardonable, indefensible.

  infamous ADJ. notorious, shocking, reprehensible, despicable, abhorrent.

  infamy N. notoriety, shamefulness, dishonorableness, disgracefulness, villainy.

  infant N. baby, child, young.

  infatuated ADJ. enamored, obsessed, enthralled, fascinated, beguiled.

  infect V. taint, transfer, poison, communicate.

  infer V. extract, conclude, deduce, gather, guess.

  inferior ADJ. common, mediocre, average, ordinary, second-rate.

infinite ADJ. eternal, boundless, endless, vast, incalculable.

infinity N. eternity, limitlessness, inexhaustibility, boundlessness.

infirmity N. sickness, disease, malady, frailty, debility, decrepitude, illness.

inflated ADJ. exaggerated, enlarged, expanded, ostentatious, pretension.

inflexible ADJ. rigid, firm, stiff, tenacious, unalterable.

inflict V. levy, impose.

• **influence** N. effect, weight, leverage, sway, control, impress. *The effect of legislation far exceeded its original intent.*

• **influential** ADJ. powerful, important, consequential, prominent. *A powerful legislator will speak on behalf of the bill.*

inform V. enlighten, notify, educate, advise, relate.

informal ADJ. easy, unofficial, regular, natural, conversational.

infrequent ADJ. rare, occasional, unusual, scarce, uncommon.

inhale V. breathe, breathe in, inspire.

inheritance N. legacy, heritage, birthright, patrimony.

• **initial** ADJ. first, primary, beginning, outset, basic, early. *The first step is often the hardest.*

initiate V. start, commence, introduce, begin, open.

injure V. hurt, impair, harm, damage, blemish.

injury N. injustice, damage, hurt, harm.

innate ADJ. native, hereditary, built-in, inborn, constitutional.

innocent ADJ. pure, clean, uncorrupted, guiltless, ignorant.

inquire V. question, ask, explore, investigate.

inquiry N. study, probe, examination, inquest, investigation.

inquisitor N. questioner, interrogator, inquirer.

insane ADJ. crazy, mad, deranged, demented, maniacal, foolish.

insanity N. madness, foolishness, mania, psychopathy, craziness, dementia.

• **insecure** ADJ. unsure, steady, shaky, unstable, nervous. *We all felt somewhat unsure about the unusual travel arrangements.*

insensible ADJ. apathetic, stolid, unfeeling, insensitive, dull, unconscious.

insincere ADJ. artificial, dishonest, false, deceitful.

insinuate V. infer, purport, hint, suggest, intimate.

insipid ADJ. banal, inane, flat, tasteless, unimaginative, bland.

• **insist** V. demand, urge, press, persevere, pressure. *A customer should demand courteous treatment.*

insolence N. impudence, rudeness, arrogance, defiance.

inspect V. search, analyze, survey, examine, investigate.

inspiration N. enthusiasm, elation, encouragement.

inspire V. stimulate, provoke, excite, encourage, prompt.

instance N. example, occurrence, illustration, case.

instant N. moment, juncture, flash, point.

instinct N. intuition, feeling, insight, talent.

instruct V. educate, teach, command, counsel, direct.

instrument N. implement, device, tool.

insubstantial ADJ. insecure, tenuous, infirm, immaterial.

insufficient ADJ. inadequate, scarce, sparse, incomplete.

insular ADJ. remote, local, provincial, protected.

intact ADJ. good, whole, entire, complete, undamaged.

integrate V. unify, consolidate, join, blend.

integrity N. character, honesty, faithfulness, soundness.

intellectual ADJ. learned, intelligent, thoughtful, insightful, sharp, precocious.

intend V. design, propose, mean, aim, conceive.

intense ADJ. furious, fierce, vehement, earnest, desperate.

intent N. meaning, intention, desire, object, motive.

- **interest** N. advantage, benefit, concern, portion. *Further education may be to your advantage.*

interfere V. obstruct, hinder, meddle, conflict, frustrate.

internal ADJ. inner, domestic, inherent, interior, intrinsic.

interpret V. decipher, unravel, translate, render, play.

- **interpretation** N. explanation, commentary, rendition, performance, execution. *Few people accepted his explanation of the events.*

interrogate V. inquire, examine, ask, interpolate, probe.

interrupt V. interfere, obstruct, suspend, stop, hinder.

intimate ADJ. confidential, close, firsthand, familiar.

intimidate V. threaten, terrify, bully, frighten, browbeat.

intolerant ADJ. bigoted, narrow, close-minded, prejudiced, biased.

intoxication N. elation, drunkenness, inebriation.

intricate ADJ. complex, involved, difficult, complicated.

intrinsic ADJ. fundamental, essential, constitutional, innate, inherent, honest, true.

introduce V. present, begin, initiate, originate, interpose, insert, preface.

intrude V. infringe, break in upon, interlope, interrupt.

intuition N. feeling, insight, instinct, impulse, guess.

invasion N. aggression, intrusion, attack, raid, foray.

inventive ADJ. innovative, creative, new, ingenious, original.

investigate V. explore, examine, inspect, analyze, study.

investigation N. exploration, examination, analysis, inspection, inquiry.

invitation N. inducement, encouragement, bid, solicitation, call.

invite V. summon, ask, court, bid, solicitate.

• **involve** V. implicate, entangle, include, entail, ensnare, imply. *Her testimony may implicate him in the robbery.*

irregular ADJ. uneven, asymmetrical, abnormal, aberrant, inconsistent.

• **irrelevant** ADJ. inapplicable, extraneous, immaterial. *Your comments are interesting but inapplicable.*

irresponsible ADJ. reckless, immature, careless, unreliable, foolish.

irritable ADJ. ill-tempered, sensitive, querulous, excitable.

irritate V. annoy, provoke, madden, disturb, inflame.

isolate V. separate, imprison, seclude, segregate.

isolated ADJ. remote, solitary, secluded, quarantined.

- **issue** N. point, subject, question, topic; offspring; —V. emanate, distribute, proceed. *I do not understand the point you are trying to make.*

item N. piece, part, detail, topic.

itinerant ADJ. unsettled, roaming, arrant, nomadic.

J

jail N. prison, reformatory, penitentiary; —V. imprison, confine.

jealous ADJ. envious, distrustful, doubtful, questioning, suspicious, possessive.

jeopardize V. endanger, threaten, imperil.

jerk V. pull, yank, twitch, shake, tug, wrench.

jinx N. hex, charm, spell, curse.

jittery ADJ. nervous, excited, uneasy, edgy, anxious.

job N. employment, function, position, career, duty.

join V. couple, connect, enroll, enlist, combine.

joint N. link, coupling, juncture.

joke N. wit, humor, wisecrack, gag, parody, prank.

journey V. trek, travel, go, voyage; —N. voyage, trip, excursion.

jovial ADJ. gay, happy, glad, joyous, cheerful, lighthearted.

joy N. ecstasy, rapture, glee, happiness, cheer.

judge V. determine, arbitrate, decide, rule, decree.

jumble V. shuffle, disorder, confuse.

jump V. leap, bound, bolt, hurdle, spring.

junction N. gathering, meeting, convergence, coupling, joining, union.

jungle N. tangle, tropics, rain forest.

just ADJ. right, deserved, appropriate, suitable, due.

justice N. fairness, equity, lawfulness, legality.

• **justify** V. defend, warrant, explain, rationalize, confirm. *You may have to defend your point of view.*

jut V. protrude, extend, bulge, overhang.

juvenile ADJ. young, childish, immature, adolescent.

K

keen ADJ. clever, sharp, enthusiastic, acute, incisive.

keep V. hold, retain, save, conserve.

kernel N. seed, heart, germ, core.

key N. answer, ticket, clue.

kick V. complain, break, boot.

kill V. murder, annihilate, finish, cancel, destroy, terminate.

kin N. relative, family, clan, kindred.

kind ADJ. tender, caring, good, benevolent, loving; —N. type, sort, variety, manner.

kindle V. arouse, provoke, light, excite, ignite.

kindness N. benevolence, grace, sympathy, goodness, generosity.

kiss V. buss, smooch, smack, brush.

knock V. wrap, hit, tap, thump.

knot V. twist, tangle, snarl; —N. twist, loop; gathering, group.

- **know** V. understand, feel, appreciate, acknowledge, comprehend. *Much of what the island natives understand cannot be translated.*

knowledge N. learning, wisdom, understanding, education, information, intelligence.

L

label N. sticker, tag, mark, stamp; —v. call, mark, classify.

labor N. work, drudgery, employment, toil, strive, travail.

laborious ADJ. difficult, hard, burdensome, arduous, tiresome.

lag V. linger, delay, loiter, falter.

lair N. hole, den, burrow, hideout.

land N. estate, acres, property, earth, homeland.

language N. speech, dialect, tongue, jargon.

languid ADJ. limp, spiritless, passive, lethargic, slothful.

lapse N. slip, error, backsliding, relapse.

larceny N. theft, stealing, embezzlement, robbery.

large ADJ. big, huge, enormous, massive, bulky, important.

lash V. strike, drive, whip, beat, goad.

lassitude N. exhaustion, stupor, apathy, lethargy, listlessness, fatigue.

last ADJ. terminal, final, concluding, closing.

late ADJ. overdue, tardy, delayed, slow, deceased.

latent ADJ. hidden, dormant, remissive, inactive.

later ADJ. subsequent, future, posterior; —ADV. after, next.

latitude N. liberty, freedom, range, breadth, scope, extent.

laud V. praise, honor, extol, esteem, merit.

laugh V. giggle, chuckle, snicker, cackle.

launch V. start, initiate, introduce, begin, drive, fire.

lavish ADJ. exorbitant, profuse, luxurious, extravagant, abundant; —V. squander, shower.

law N. measure, legislation, enactment, ordinance, edict, theorem, principle, axiom.

lawful ADJ. legal, legitimate, permitted, allowable, authorized.

lawless ADJ. illegal, disobedient, illicit, prohibited, lax, negligent, tolerant, careless, loose, unobservant.

lay V. set, place, put.

laziness N. loafing, sloth, sluggishness, idleness, dormancy, lethargy.

lazy ADJ. lethargic, sluggish, dormant, slow, inactive, slothful, sleepy.

lead V. guide, conduct, oversee, precede, direct, regulate.

leader N. chief, boss, director, guide, commander, conductor.

league N. conference, union, class, alliance.

lean V. incline, tend, bend, slant, hang.

leap V. jump, spring, vault, bound, romp.

learn V. gain, acquire, study, discover, master.

leave V. go, part, quit, desert, vacate.

legalize V. legitimize, allow, authorize, permit, warrant.

legend N. myth, lore, fable, tradition.

legitimacy N. legality, truth, validity, authenticity.

leisure N. rest, freedom, relaxation, vacation, ease.

lend V. loan, advance, supply, give.

length N. limit, extreme, reach, extent, distance.

lengthen V. prolong, extend, stretch, increase.

let V. allow, permit, authorize, grant.

lethargic ADJ. sluggish, lazy, listless, slow, apathetic.

letter N. note, epistle, missive, literalness.

level ADJ. flat, uniform, even, horizontal, smooth; —V. destroy, flatten, demolish, equalize.

levy V. charge; —N. tax, duty, draft.

liable ADJ. accountable, responsible, susceptible, subject to, likely, vulnerable.

liar N. perjurer, storyteller, fabricator.

liberal ADJ. progressive, left, fair, broad, generous.

liberty N. privilege, right, freedom, latitude, license.

license V. warrant, permit, approve. authorize; — N. liberty, permission.

lie V. fabricate, falsify, deceive, repose, recline.

life N. existence, nature, vitality, duration, entity, lifespan, longevity.

lift V. elevate, raise, hoist, recall, revoke.

light N. illumination, brightness, radiation; —V. brighten, illuminate, animate, ignite, fire.

light-headed ADJ. dizzy, giddy, vertiginous, silly, faint.

lighthearted ADJ. gay, happy, cheerful, glad.

like V. admire, fancy, enjoy; —ADJ. analogous, similar, equivalent.

liken V. equate, compare, analogize, favor.

likeness N. analogy, similarity, comparison, affinity.

• **limit** N. boundary, maximum, extreme, length; —V. restrict, confine. *It was necessary to place some boundary on their investigation.*

limp V., N. hobble, stagger; —ADJ. soft, flexible, limber.

limpid ADJ. transparent, clear, translucent, pure, bright.

line N. row, succession, file, cord, string, rope, program, policy.

linger V. hesitate, delay, loiter, remain, pause.

link V. join, connect, combine, associate.

liquidate V. eliminate, annihilate, terminate, settle, pay, kill.

list N. catalog, schedule, record.

listen V. hear, attend, mark, heed, hark, pay attention to.

literal ADJ. verbatim, actual, exact, true, rigorous.

little ADJ. small, petite, unimportant, trivial, insignificant.

livable ADJ. inhabitable, bearable, cozy, occupiable.

live V. reside, dwell, exist, be, survive, inhabit.

lively ADJ. animated, vivacious, spirited, happy, active.

living N. support, sustenance, livelihood, alimony; —ADJ. alive, existing.

load N. cargo, burden, weight; —V. charge, fill, heap.

loathing N. hate, disgust, abhorrence, disapproval, condemnation.

loathsome ADJ. offensive, filthy, abominable, foul, obnoxious.

local ADJ. limited, restricted, isolated, narrow, narrow-minded, parochial, provincial.

locale N. scene, locality, environment.

locality N. place, region, location, area, vicinity.

locate V. find, discover, position, place, situate.

location N. point, position, spot, place, site.

lofty ADJ. airy, elevated, exalted, towering, high.

• **logic** N. reason, sense, rationality, coherence, validity. *Her speech appealed to reason more than emotion.*

loiter V. stall, linger, idle, delay.

lone ADJ. separate, sole, solitary, deserted, secluded.

lonely ADJ. depressed, friendless, lonesome, deserted, desolate.

lonesome ADJ. alone, desolate, isolated, solitary.

long ADJ. lengthy, elongated, extended, tedious, prolonged.

longing N. dream, desire, yearning.

look V. survey, glance, see, regard, watch, observe.

lookout N. outlook, guard, observatory, sentry.

loose ADJ., ADV. untied, unrestrained, free, relaxed.

loosen V. untie, undo, ease, unfasten.

loot N. booty, plunder; —V. plunder, ransack, steal, rob.

lore N. myth, tradition, folklore, superstition, fable.

lorn ADJ. lonely, abandoned, solitary.

lose V. misplace, mislay, waste.

lost ADJ. missing, gone, absent, vanished.

lot N. plot, parcel; fate, fortune; gathering, assemblage, group.

loud ADJ. resonant, deafening, roaring, clamorous, noisy.

love N. amour, passion, emotion, tenderness, friendship, devotion, attraction, warmth.

low ADJ. deep, depressed, sunken, shameless, disgraceful, base.

lowly ADJ. humble, common, poor, unimportant, submissive.

loyal ADJ. faithful, devoted, trustworthy, steadfast.

lucid ADJ. clear, serene, transparent, pure, rational, explicit, plain, evident.

• **luck** N. fortune, chance, success, fate. *He had the good fortune to win the lottery.*

luminary N. dignitary, celebrity, star.

lump N. hunk, chunk, clump, wad, clod, lug.

lurch V. tilt, roll, stumble, stagger, falter, reel, wobble.

lure V. tempt, attract, entice, bait, delude.

lurid ADJ. pale, horrible, ghastly, gruesome.

luscious ADJ. delightful, pleasing, delicious, satisfying, appetizing.

lush ADJ. succulent, abundant, fresh, opulent, profuse.

lust V. desire, hunger; —N. craving, thirst, passion, avarice.

lustrous ADJ. eminent, glossy, shining, brilliant, bright, glowing.

lusty ADJ. vigorous, robust, strong, vital.

luxuriant ADJ. profuse, abundant, thick, fruitful, rich.

luxurious ADJ. opulent, plush, extravagant, posh, lavish.

M

mad ADJ. insane, foolish, angry, upset, wild, frenzied, enthusiastic.

made-up ADJ. fictitious, invented, assumed.

madness N. insanity, lunacy, psychosis, paranoia.

magic N. sorcery, wizardry, alchemy, enchantment, occultism, witchcraft.

magnanimous ADJ. generous, noble, exalted, charitable, honorable.

magnetic ADJ. attractive, charismatic.

magnification N. amplification, enlargement, exaggeration.

magnificent ADJ. excellent, sublime, outstanding, glorious, grand.

magnify V. amplify, enlarge, exalt, honor, exaggerate, aggrandize.

magnitude N. degree, bulk, size, greatness, volume.

main ADJ. primary, principal, leading, foremost.

maintain V. defend, claim, sustain, assert, justify.

make V. construct, form, do, fabricate, produce, prepare.

makeout V. discern, understand, recognize, perceive.

maker N. originator, creator, builder.

maladroit ADJ. unskillful, clumsy, tactless, inept, awkward.

malady N. disease, illness, ailment, infirmity.

male ADJ. manlike, masculine, virile.

malevolent ADJ. evil, spiteful, malicious, mean, hateful.

malfunction V. misbehave, act up, fail.

malice N. hatred, spite, malevolence, resentment, bitterness.

malign V. slander, libel, defame, discredit.

malleable ADJ. flexible, ductile, pliable, workable.

man N. male, mankind, human being.

• **manage** V. guide, conduct, rule, administer, get by, fend. *Frank can guide the company into the future.*

management N. guidance, control, direction, administration, conservation.

manager N. executive, supervisor, boss, administrator, director.

maneuver N. movement, tactic, plot, procedure, artifice.

mania N. insanity, enthusiasm, rage, madness.

maniac N. madman, lunatic, nut.

manifest V. show, embody, express; —ADJ. clear, apparent, evident, obvious.

manifestation N. sign, display.

manipulate V. direct, control, exploit, conduct, handle, engineer.

• **mankind** N. humanity, people, men, men and women. *The future of humanity may be at stake.*

man-made ADJ. artificial, synthetic, invented, manufactured.

manner N. custom, habit, behavior, style, bearing.

manners N. etiquette, civilities, behavior, demeanor, formalities.

many ADJ. diverse, numerous, myriad, legion, several.

map V., N. plot, chart, design, diagram, graph.

march V. walk, parade, step, stride, move.

margin N. edge, border, limit, fringe, minimum.

marine ADJ. nautical, oceanic, seagoing, naval.

marital ADJ. matrimonial, nuptial, conjugal, espousal.

mark N. imprint, stamp, impression, symbol, dent, stain, scratch, mar.

marriage N. wedding, matrimony, conjugality, espousal, wedlock, union.

married ADJ. wedded, espoused.

marry V. wed, espouse, mate.

martial ADJ. military, warlike, combative, belligerent.

marvel N. sensation, wonder, prodigy, miracle.

marvelous ADJ. wondrous, phenomenal, extraordinary, fabulous, amazing, astounding, incredible.

mask V. disguise, cover, veil, hide, masquerade.

masquerade V. pose, disguise, veil, trick.

mass N. bulk, body, total, whole, amount.

masses N. commonality, people, magnitude, crowds.

massive ADJ. immense, gigantic, weighty, huge, heavy, colossal.

master N. expert, chief, savant, sage, commander, patriarch; —V. learn, triumph, domesticate, tame.

masterful ADJ. dictatorial, authoritative, commanding, artful, expert.

masterly ADJ. skillful, expert, adroit.

masterpiece N. accomplishment, monument, tour de force.

mastery N. dominance, skill, power, ascendancy, grasp.

match N. equivalent, equal, mate, competitor, contest, rivalry; —V. equate, balance, liken.

mate N. spouse, friend, companion; —V. match, associate.

material N. matter, substance, fabric, cloth; — ADJ. substantial, real, tangible.

materialistic ADJ. earthly, carnal, worldly, mundane.

materialize V. embody, appear, realize.

• **matter** N. substance, material, thing, affair, subject. *We identified the unusual substance.*

mature ADJ. experienced, aged, adult, ripe; —V. grow, develop, ripen, age.

maxim N. precept, proverb, adage, epigram, tenet, teaching.

maximum ADJ. greatest, largest, supreme, utmost; —N. crest, climax, ultimate, top.

• **maybe** ADV. perhaps, possibly, perchance. *Perhaps it will rain tomorrow.*

meager ADJ. thin, small, slender, deficit, slight.

mean V. intend, denote, express, state; —ADJ. malevolent, vile, ignoble, despicable.

meander V. wander, ramble, drift, stroll.

• **meaning** N. significance, message, intention, purport. *She explained the significance of the data.*

• **meaningful** ADJ. important, pregnant, reasonable, expressive. *They made an important contribution to the project.*

means N. instrument, medium, channel, agent, method, system, resources, manner.

measure N. volume, dimension, degree, standard, rule; —V. gauge, estimate, rule, weigh.

measured ADJ. rhythmical, deliberate, limited, finite.

meat N. flesh, animal, food.

meddle V. interfere, intrude, tamper, annoy.

media N. press, radio, television.

median ADJ. average, medium.

medication N. drug, medicine, prescription, potion.

medicine N. drug, medication, prescription, potion, treatment.

meditate V. think, ponder, contemplate, consider, ruminate.

medium N. compromise, average, mean, environment, surrounding, channel, material.

meek ADJ. gentle, humble, unassuming, modest, calm, bashful.

meet V. encounter, intersect, converge, rendezvous, greet.

meeting N. assembly, reunion, convention, conference, junction.

melancholy ADJ. sad, depressed, gloomy, despondent, grim, doleful, joyless, blue.

melodious ADJ. agreeable, harmonious, pleasing, tuneful, musical.

melodramatic ADJ. theatric, dramatic, corny, sentimental.

melody N. tune, theme, aria, air.

melt V. dissolve, vanish, blend, liquefy.

memorial N. commemoration, remembrance, record, monument.

memorize V. learn, retain, remember.

memory N. recollection, reminiscence, remembrance, retention.

menace N. danger, hazard, threat; —V. threaten, endanger, intimidate.

mend V. fix, restore, collect, improve, recover.

• **mental** ADJ. intellectual, cerebral, psychological.
His intellectual abilities are particularly admirable.

mentality N. psychology, intelligence, state of mind.

mention V. refer, name, note, allude, cite.

mentor N. instructor, advisor, teacher, guide.

merciful ADJ. tolerant, kind, tender, benevolent, gentle, gracious.

merciless ADJ. remorseless, unmerciful, cruel, hard, savage.

mere ADJ. scant, bare, very.

merely ADJ. only, barely, hardly, just.

merit N. value, quality, worth, virtue, perfection.

merry ADJ. cheerful, happy, gay, joyous, gleeful, spritely.

mess N. disorder, confusion, jumble, melange, combination, mixture.

message N. communication, dispatch, letter, signal, report.

metaphor N. allegory, symbol, analogy, comparison, allusion, simile.

metamorphosis N. transformation, change, conversion.

metaphysical ADJ. abstract, supernatural, immaterial, subjective, psychological.

method N. system, pattern, order, style, way.

meticulous ADJ. precise, careful, exacting, clean.

middle ADJ. central, average, axial, median, intermediate; center, midpoint, core.

might N. authority, strength, force, power, vigor.

mighty ADJ. great, forceful, strong, powerful, omnipotent, vigorous, robust.

migrant ADJ. transitory, itinerant, immigrant, nomadic, emigrant, transient.

migrate V. emigrate, immigrate, move, relocate, resettle.

mild ADJ. temperate, gentle, calm, moderate,

kind, peaceful.

military ADJ. marital, warlike, militaristic, bellicose.

mimicry N. imitation, mockery, simulation, parody.

mind N. intellect, reason, belief, psychology, intention, liking, inclination; —V. care, look, follow, notice.

mindful ADJ. alert, aware, attentive, careful, observant.

mindless ADJ. senseless, foolish, irrational, meaningless, pointless, insane.

mingle V. socialize, mix, combine, blend.

minimal ADJ. essential, basic, fundamental, smallest.

• **minimum** ADJ. least, smallest, minimal, margin. *The alternative school required the least amount of discipline.*

minor ADJ. inferior, lesser, subordinate, younger, lower, secondary.

minority N. ethnic group, race.

minute ADJ. small, detailed, minuscule, tiny; —N. instant, moment, second.

miracle N. marvel, wonder, prodigy.

miraculous ADJ. wonderful, marvelous, extraordinary, spectacular, fabulous.

mirror V. reflect, echo.

misadventure N. mishap, accident, catastrophe, disaster; victory, good fortune, triumph.

misapprehension N. misunderstanding, mistake, misinterpretation.

misbehave V. malfunction, cut up, act up, carry on.

miscalculate V. misfigure, misjudge.

miscellaneous ADJ. combined, various, motley, confused, mixed, mingled.

mischief N. injury, detriment, harm, grievance, roguishness.

• **misconception** N. misunderstanding, misinterpretation, misapprehension. *Their actions were unfortunately based on a misunderstanding.*

misconstrue V. misunderstand, misconceive, mistake, misinterpret, misjudge, misread.

miscue N. error, mistake, blunder.

miser N. scrooge, tightwad, hoarder, skimper, cheapskate.

miserable ADJ. woeful, wretched, pained, sorrowful, unhappy, sick, depressed.

misery N. unhappiness, pain, sorrow, affliction, anguish, grief, despondency.

misfortune N. bad luck, adversity, accident, injury, calamity.

mishandle V. botch, abuse, mistreat.

misjudge V. miscalculate, err, misconstrue, overshoot.

mismanage V. botch, mishandle, misbehave.

misplace V. lose, displace.

misrepresent V. exaggerate, misstate, feign, pervert, falsify, distort.

miss V. desire, crave, want, need, yearn for, drop, fumble.

mission N. affair, purpose, errand, activity.

misstep N. error, mistake.

mist N. haze, fog, cloud.

- **mistake** N. error, oversight, failure, flaw. *One error is certainly forgivable.*

mistrust V. suspect, fear, distrust; —N. doubt, suspicion.

misunderstand V. disagree, misinterpret, misapprehend, misconstrue.

misuse V. abuse, exploit, manipulate, take advantage of.

mix V. blend, combine, fuse, merge, stir, mingle.

mixture N. blend, amalgam, fusion, compound.

mob N. crowd, gang, swarm, horde.

mobile ADJ. transportable, movable, free.

mobilize V. organize, drive, rally, marshal.

mock V. imitate, ridicule, scorn, jeer.

mode N. fashion, style, method, manner, condition.

model N. pattern, example, miniature, imitation, copy, style, version, shape, form, design, mold.

moderate ADJ. reasonable, temperate, fair, judicious, calm, modest.

moderation N. temperance, measure, calm.

modern ADJ. new, recent, current, contemporary.

modest ADJ. retiring, shy, bashful, reserved, diffident.

modesty N. humility, diffidence, humbleness, simplicity, chastity.

modify V. change, alter, convert, transform.

moist ADJ. damp, humid, watery, soaked, wet, dank.

mold V. make, shape form, cast, model.

moment N. minute, flash, second, instant.

momentary ADJ. impending, imminent, transitory.

momentous ADJ. serious, important, consequential, critical, eventful, memorable.

• **money** N. wealth, gold, riches, notes, coins, greenbacks, bills, treasure. *Happiness does not depend primarily upon wealth.*

monopoly N. restriction, limitation, syndicate, corner, cartel, combination.

monotony N. tediousness, tedium, boredom, uniformity, monotone, ennui.

monster N. freak, fiend, beast, demon, brute.

monstrous ADJ. huge, enormous, immense, incredible, shocking, outrageous, horrible, awful.

mood N. temper, spirit, disposition, emotion.

moody ADJ. temperamental, excitable, whimsical, mercurial, fickle.

moor V. attach, anchor, fasten.

moral ADJ. honest, ethical, honorable, upright, elevated.

morale N. confidence, esprit, assurance.

morality N. good, ethic.

morals N. values, ethics.

morbid ADJ. sick, morose, melancholic, unwholesome, macabre.

more ADJ. additional, extra; —ADV. better, additionally.

morsel N. piece, bit, bite.

mortal ADJ. human, earthly, temporary, fatal, deadly.

• **mostly** ADV. mainly, generally, principally, largely, chiefly. *The participants were mainly from California.*

motion N. change, movement, gesture, action.

• **motivate** V. stimulate, encourage, provoke, prompt. *This incentive should stimulate interest among the sales force.*

motive N. purpose, reason, cause.

mount V. climb, ascend, read, prepare.

mountain N. ridge, peak, mount.

move V. shift, transfer, advance, relocate, stir, provoke; —N. motion, tactic, procedure, maneuver.

moving ADJ. emotional, affecting, touching.

muddle N. dilemma, confusion, disorder, turmoil, difficulty; —V. confuse, perturb, mix, shuffle.

muffle V. conceal, deaden, soften, mute, stifle.

mundane ADJ. terrestrial, worldly, everyday, earthly.

murder V. kill, slay, execute, assassinate.

murmur V. whisper, sigh, mumble, mutter.

muscular ADJ. sturdy, robust, strong, powerful, brawny.

musical ADJ. melodious, lyrical, euphonic, melodic, harmonious.

must V. need to, have to, obligated to.

mute ADJ. speechless, silent, dumb, soundless, still.

mutter V. whisper, murmur, mumble, grumble.

mutual ADJ. joint, reciprocal, common, shared, identical.

mysterious ADJ. enigmatic, obscure, mystic, dark, unexplainable, ambiguous, strange.

mystery N. puzzle, enigma, conundrum.

myth N. fable, vision, allegory, fantasy, creation.

N

nab V. catch, trap, arrest, grab, snag.

naked ADJ. bare, nude, exposed, uncovered.

name N. title, appellation, designation, character, reputation; —V. call, designate, term, entitle, mention, cite, appoint.

nap N. doze, siesta, catnap, snooze, rest; —V. doze, slumber.

narrow ADJ. thin, cramped, restricted, confined, limited, small.

narrow-minded ADJ. bigoted, close-minded, intolerant, prejudiced.

nasty ADJ. offensive, disagreeable, mean, obscene, foul, dirty.

nation N. republic, commonwealth, society, people, country.

native ADJ. indigenous, original, natural, innate, hereditary, inherent.

- **natural** ADJ. customary, characteristic, usual, normal, hereditary, innate, organic, pure. *It was customary that the guest should be given a place at the table.*

- **nature** N. character, disposition, variety, kind, universe, world, essence. *We relied upon her character as an assertive personality in electing her president.*

naughty ADJ. disobedient, contrary, bad, mischievous, rowdy.

near ADJ. adjoining, close, adjacent, bordering, neighboring.

nearby ADJ. convenient, close, neighboring, adjacent, proximal.

neat ADJ. trim, orderly, tidy, well-organized, clean.

• **necessary** ADJ. required, needed, essential, indispensable. *Attendance is required.*

• **necessity** N. condition, need, requirement, prerequisite. *Proof of your college education is a condition of your employment.*

need V. want, require, lack; —N. necessity, requirement, poverty, want.

nefarious ADJ. evil, wicked, corrupt, sinister, vile, depraved.

negate V. abolish, revoke, nullify, deny.

neglect V. ignore, disregard, overlook, omit; —N. omission, oversight, negligence, disregard.

negligent ADJ. derelict, neglectful, remiss, lax.

negligible ADJ. trivial, remote, petty, insignificant, unimportant.

negotiate V. confer, bargain, arrange, contract.

neighborhood N. quarter, area, environs, vicinity, community.

nervous ADJ. anxious, edgy, timid, restless, excitable, afraid.

neutral ADJ. unbiased, nonpartisan, impartial, unprejudiced, colorless, bland, impersonal, detached.

new ADJ. fresh, original, recent, modern, novel.

- **nice** ADJ. pleasing, attractive, agreeable, pleasant, friendly, kind, thoughtful. *The innkeeper had a pleasing face.*

night N. evening, darkness, dusk, nighttime.

noble ADJ. honorable, virtuous, dignified, aristocratic, elevated.

noise N. uproar, racket, clamor, outcry.

nomadic ADJ. vagabond, roaming, migrant, wandering, vagrant.

nonchalant ADJ. indifferent, careless, relaxed, cool, casual, composed.

- **nonsense** N. absurdity, insanity, pretense, senselessness, folly. *We have no time for such absurdity.*

nosy ADJ. curious, prying, intrusive, inquisitive.

notable ADJ. remarkable, unusual, renowned, eminent, distinguished.

note V. observe, view, remark, notice, perceive; —N. comment, letter, acknowledgment, memorandum, message.

- **nothing** N. nil, nonentity, zero, obscurity, nothingness. *Our influence over their actions was nil.*

notice V. perceive, detect, note, observe; —N. bulletin, notification, announcement, note.

noticeable ADJ. outstanding, prominent, obvious, evident, noteworthy, apparent.

notoriety N. fame, infamy.

notorious ADJ. infamous, disreputable, arrant, shameful.

novelty N. innovation, originality, freshness.

novice N. beginner, newcomer, amateur, student, learner.

now ADV. today, currently, actually, directly, periodically.

nude ADJ. unclothed, naked, bare, stripped, uncovered.

numb ADJ. dull, dead, paralyzed, insensitive, unfeeling.

numerate V. count, enumerate, add, compute, calculate.

nurse V. nurture, nourish, foster, tend, suckle.

nutritious ADJ. healthful, alimentary.

O

obedience N. compliance, submission, respect, acquiescence.

obedient ADJ. loyal, compliant, submissive, faithful, respectful.

obese ADJ. fat, stout, portly, plump, chubby, corpulent.

object N. item, article, thing, goal; —V. protest, disapprove.

• **objection** N. protest, challenge, disapproval. *The coach lodged a formal protest against the umpire.*

objective N. goal, intention, aim, destination, aspiration; —ADJ. realistic, impartial, unbiased, fair, just.

obligation N. duty, responsibility, debt, requirement, contract.

oblige V. force, compel, insist, benefit, help, favor.

obliged ADJ. forced, required, bound, grateful, pleased, thankful.

oblique ADJ. indirect, biased, crooked, devious, diagonal, slanting.

obliterate V. delete, cancel, erase.

obnoxious ADJ. offensive, loathsome, filthy, reprehensible, displeasing.

obscene ADJ. lewd, vulgar, crude, pornographic.

obscenity N. filth, dirt, smut, indecency, lewdness, profanity.

obscure ADJ. mysterious, dark, complex, ambiguous.

observance N. ceremony, celebration, obedience, watch.

observation N. remark, comment, notice, opinion.

observe V. regard, watch, witness, look, obey, celebrate, honor.

obsess V. possess, haunt.

obsolete ADJ. archaic, outdated, superseded, old-fashioned, antique.

obstacle N. barricade, hindrance, bar, difficulty, impediment.

obstinate ADJ. resolute, stubborn, opinionated, willful, determined.

obstruct V. hinder, block, impede, prevent, stop.

obtain V. acquire, get, attain, achieve.

- **obvious** ADJ. apparent, unmistakable, plain, visible, clear. *Typographical errors were apparent throughout the term paper.*

occasion N. occurrence, event, happening, opportunity.

occasional ADJ. random, intermittent, infrequent, sporadic.

occupation N. profession, business, employment, work, vocation, job.

occupy V. inhabit, fill, seize, possess.

- **occur** V. happen, befall, take place. *Something may happen at any moment.*

odd ADJ. curious, strange, bizarre, extraordinary.

oddity N. strangeness, eccentricity, characteristic, exception, mystery, peculiarity.

odds N. chance, luck, advantage.

odious ADJ. foul, abhorrent, hateful, filthy, disgusting.

odor N. scent, aroma, smell, essence.

off ADJ. wrong, erroneous; remote, removed from.

offend V. anger, provoke, annoy, irritate, insult.

offense N. crime, transgression, attack; wrong, insult.

offensive ADJ. insulting, discourteous, revolting, loathsome, repulsive, disgusting.

offer V. propose, suggest, volunteer, present.

office N. bureau, study, post, position, occupation.

official ADJ. authentic, reliable, authoritative, genuine.

offset V. compensate, counteract, balance, neutralize.

OK ADV. all right, yes; —ADJ. all right, acceptable; —V. permit, give permission.

old-fashioned ADJ. archaic, vintage, old, dated, antique.

omen N. sign, mark, forewarning, auspice.

ominous ADJ. fateful, imminent, threatening, foreboding.

omit V. exclude, drop, forget, disregard, overlook.

one ADJ. lone, single, solitary.

oneness N. unity, sameness, completeness, wholeness.

only ADV. merely, simply, solely, exclusively, just.

onset N. opening, commencement, beginning, attack.

open ADJ. public, accessible, unclosed, frank, clear, straightforward, indefinite, ambiguous; —V. unlock, begin, expand.

opening N. hole, gap, door, start, beginning, opportunity, vacancy.

operate V. run, perform, handle, conduct, work, use.

operation N. execution, action, process, maneuver.

operator N. driver, pilot, aviator, designer, schemer.

opportune ADJ. timely, proper, suitable, appropriate, favorable.

• **opportunity** N. chance, freedom, latitude, occasion. *The emigrants were given the chance to begin new careers.*

oppose V. counteract, resist, combat, contest.

opposite ADJ. reverse, contrary, contradictory, converse.

opposition N. resistance, antagonism, defiance, adversary, contestant.

oppress V. persecute, depress, burden, crush, afflict.

optimism N. hope, confidence, assuredness, cheer, enthusiasm.

optimistic ADJ. hopeful, confident, assured, enthusiastic, positive.

• **option** N. recourse, choice, remedy, alternative. *We have little recourse but to sue.*

optional ADJ. elective, discretionary, alternative.

opulent ADJ. wealthy, luxurious, profuse, rich, plentiful.

oral ADJ. vocal, verbal, spoken, voiced.

oratorical ADJ. rhetorical, declamatory, elocutionary.

orb N. globe, sphere, circle, eye.

order N. instruction, command, direction, requirement, regulation, union, hierarchy, class; —V. instruct, command, arrange.

orderly ADJ. regular, neat, methodical, tidy.

• **ordinary** ADJ. common, plain, average, typical, regular. *The movie will appeal most to common tastes.*

organ N. means, branch.

organic ADJ. natural, pure, essential, inherent, fundamental.

• **organize** V. plan, establish, arrange, institute. *She spent more than a week trying to plan the district meeting.*

origin N. commencement, source, beginning, route, derivation, ancestry.

- **original** ADJ. first, primary, fresh, new, inventive, creative, unique. *I liked the first version of your essay.*

originate V. begin, arise, invent, create.

ornament N. adornment, decoration, embellishment, beautification.

orthodox ADJ. standard, strict, conforming, sanctioned, received.

outburst N. explosion, eruption, outbreak, blowup.

outcry N. scream, exclamation, shout, protest, uproar.

outfit V. supply, equip, clothe; —N. gear, equipment, clothing, material.

outline V. plan, delineate, draft, sketch; —N. profile, draft, plan, delineation.

outlook N. point of view, view, opinion, chance, opportunity, future.

outrage N. crime, indignity, abuse, injury, insult.

outrageous ADJ. flagrant, enormous, unreasonable, preposterous.

outspoken ADJ. forthright, candid, vocal, direct, unreserved.

- **outstanding** ADJ. magnificent, exceptional, eminent, notable, prominent. *We visited a magnificent cathedral.*

outwit V. trick, outsmart, outmaneuver, hoax.

overbearing ADJ. oppressive, domineering, arrogant, proud, dictatorial.

overblown ADJ. inflated, exaggerated, fat.

overcast ADJ. clouded, dark, obscure, cloudy.

overcome V. defeat, conquer, triumph, overwhelm.

overhaul V. fix, rebuild, revamp, recondition.

overjoyed ADJ. elated, happy, gleeful, delighted.

overlook V. neglect, ignore, disregard, supervise, dominate.

oversize ADJ. bulky, big, enormous.

overthrow V. topple, remove, destroy, overturn.

overturn V. topple, overthrow, upset, conquer.

overwhelm V. inundate, overpower, crush, defeat.

own V. hold, have, control, possess.

owner N. proprietor, possessor, holder.

ownership N. possession, title, dominion.

P

pace N. velocity, rate, speed, stride.

pacifist ADJ. peaceable, nonviolent; —N. conscientious objector.

pacify V. quiet, calm, appease, tranquilize, placate.

pack V. fill, stuff, cram, crowd, press.

pact N. treaty, agreement, covenant.

pain N. discomfort, suffering, affliction, distress.

painful ADJ. torturous, agonizing, sharp, piercing, excruciating.

pair N. couple, duo, twosome, team, match.

pale ADJ. colorless, white, pallid, faint, dim.

palpitate V. beat, flutter, vibrate, pulsate, throb.

panic N. terror, fright, harm, fear, horror.

pant V. gasp, wheeze, heave, huff.

parade N. procession, march, festival, display.

paradigm N. model, pattern, ideal.

paradise N. heaven, utopia, nirvana.

parallel ADJ. congruent, collateral, alike, analogous.

paralyze V. shock, astound, stun, numb, stupefy, disable, immobilize.

paraphrase V. explain, restate, reword, translate.

parasite N. sponge, leech, sycophant, dependent, bloodsucker.

pardonable ADJ. forgivable, excusable, reprievable, condonable.

parody N. mockery, caricature, imitation, mimicry, satire, takeoff.

part N. section, fragment, component, division, piece.

partake V. participate, contribute, join, eat.

partial ADJ. biased, prejudiced, unfair, fragmentary, imperfect.

partiality N. bias, preference, prejudice, leaning, favoritism.

participant N. partner, actor, player.

• **participate** V. partake, join, indulge, engage.
Everyone is invited to partake in the Thanksgiving meal.

particular ADJ. definite, precise, specific, exact, meticulous, discriminating.

partition N. separation, barrier, division, wall.

partner N. associate, colleague, spouse, companion.

party N. troop, company, league, band, gala, festivity.

pass V. convey, hand, approve, accept, adopt, transcend, surpass, overcome.

passage N. rate, entrance, confirmation, proof, verse, stanza.

passion N. ecstasy, zeal, dedication, devotion, infatuation, desire.

passionate ADJ. vehement, earnest, intense, ardent, erotic.

passive ADJ. submissive, yielding, resigned, acquiescent, compliant.

past ADJ. previous, former, precedent, late.

patch V. repair, fix, mend, restore.

patience N. composure, perseverance, endurance, forbearance, resignation.

patron N. advocate, supporter, benefactor, contributor, customer, client, buyer.

patronage N. business, trade, traffic, sponsorship, backing, clientele.

patronize V. support, sponsor, condescend, mock.

pattern N. guide, example, model, method, habit, form, figure.

pause V. hesitate, linger, rest, wait, discontinue.

pawn N. tool, puppet, stooge, instrument.

pay V. recompense, compensate, settle, reward.

peaceable ADJ. tranquil, calm, nonviolent, friendly, pacifist.

peak N. height, summit, top, climax, crest.

pedagogy N. learning, education, scholarship, teaching, instruction.

pejorative ADJ. degrading, disparaging, deprecatory.

penalty N. sanction, fine, punishment.

penetrate V. perforate, puncture, enter, pierce.

penitence N. atonement, remorse, attrition, distress, angst, grief, sorrow.

pensive ADJ. speculative, thoughtful, reflective, solemn, meditative.

• **people** N. community, population, humanity, persons, public. *The proposed zoning changes should be approved by the community.*

perceive V. observe, discern, note, distinguish, feel, sense.

perceptible ADJ. tangible, visible, noticeable, detectable, discernible, appreciable.

perception N. awareness, insight, recognition, cognizance, acumen.

perfect ADJ. flawless, impeccable, absolute, ideal.

perforate V. puncture, penetrate, breach, pierce.

perform V. execute, do, complete, achieve, fulfill.

performance N. interpretation, execution, fulfillment, show, entertainment.

period N. stage, phase, interval, duration, span, season.

periphery N. circumference, border, boundary, edge.

permissible ADJ. allowable, admissible, legal, permitted.

permission N. freedom, consent, license, authority, permit.

permit V. consent, allow, authorize, let, approve.

perpetual ADJ. incessant, continual, constant, endless.

perplex V. confound, complicate, mystify, confuse, bewilder, puzzle.

persevere V. endure, continue, insist, carry on, survive.

persist V. persevere, endure, stay, try.

- **personal** ADJ. private, secret, intimate, individual. *Some matters were too private to discuss.*

personify V. represent, embody.

perspective N. view, viewpoint, opinion, point of view.

persuade V. convince, convert, influence, prompt, urge.

persuasion N. faith, religion, belief, influence.

persuasive ADJ. influential, convincing, suave, agreeable.

pertain V. belong, apply.

pertinent ADJ. relevant, fitting, applicable, apropos.

pervade V. penetrate, fill, permeate, saturate, infiltrate.

pervert V. corrupt, distort, abuse.

pessimist N. cynic, misanthrope, foreboder, defeatist.

petite ADJ. little, tiny, small, diminutive.

petty ADJ. trivial, insignificant, small, inconsequential, insignificant, irrelevant.

phase N. period, side, facet, stage, view.

phenomenal ADJ. wonderful, fabulous, marvelous, miraculous.

phenomenon N. event, marvel, occurrence, happening, incident.

phrase N. wording, sentence, expression; —V. word, formulate, express.

• **physical** ADJ. tangible, corporeal, material, sensual, bodily, carnal. *He was booked on tangible evidence, not supposition.*

pick V. select, choose, gather, cull, harvest.

picture N. photograph, representation, illustration, drawing; —V. imagine, envision, depict.

picturesque ADJ. scenic, colorful, beautiful, pictorial, pleasing.

piece N. part, section, segment, bit, fraction.

pierce V. perforate, cut, puncture, penetrate.

pile N. collection, stack, heap.

pillage V. rob, spoil, plunder, sack, destroy, loot.

pilot N. captain, aviator, guide; —V. guide, steer, drive.

pinch N. difficulty, predicament, strain, squeeze.

pinnacle N. summit, apex, climax, culmination, peak.

pinpoint V. locate, fix, place, find.

pioneer N. adventurer, colonist, builder, settler, founder.

pitch V. throw, toss, incline, grade, angle.

pitfall N. peril, hazard, risk, snare, danger, trap.

pity N. sympathy, compassion, empathy, mercy, kindness.

pivotal ADJ. critical, crucial, focal, key, essential.

- **place** N. area, spot, region, location; —V. set, put, position. *We visited an area known for frequent earthquakes.*

placid ADJ. calm, quiet, undisturbed, gentle, serene.

plague V. curse, annoy, trouble, irritate.

plain ADJ. obvious, clear, simple, apparent, modest, unattractive.

plan V. plot, scheme, conspire, devise; —N., V. design, sketch, diagram, chart; —N. method, approach, device.

planet N. orb, earth, globe.

plant V. sew, seed, put, place.

plastic ADJ. synthetic, artificial, flexible, ductile, pliant.

plausible ADJ. acceptable, believable, likely, justifiable, probable, credible.

play V. frolic, romp, perform, show.

player N. actor, performer, musician.

plea N. excuse, request, appeal, supplication.

pleasant ADJ. enjoyable, agreeable, pleasing, amusing, comforting.

please V. satisfy, delight, suit, gratify.

- **pleasing** ADJ. pleasant, agreeable, enjoyable, pleasurable. *The weather remained pleasant throughout June.*

pleasurable ADJ. satisfying, enjoyable, pleasing, delightful, agreeable.

pleasure N. joy, delight, satisfaction, happiness, ecstasy, rapture.

pledge V. commit, promise; —N. contract, vow, guarantee.

plentiful ADJ. profuse, ample, full, generous, rich, sufficient, abundant.

plenty N. abundance, plenitude, fullness; —ADJ. ample, plentiful.

pliable ADJ. malleable, flexible, lithe, supple, ductile.

plod V. trudge, wade, grind, stomp, toil.

plot N. story, intrigue, theme, design, plan.

plunge V. fall, dive, immerse, submerge, jump.

poem N. verse, poetry, rhyme, lyric.

poet N. muse, bard, writer, author.

poignant ADJ. affecting, intense, sharp, piercing.

- **point** N. tip, apex, end, location, position, place; —V. direct, aim, indicate, show. *He touched the tip of the needle carefully to his finger.*

- **point of view** N. perspective, outlook, opinion, viewpoint, angle. *We all want to hear your perspective on the issue.*

poise N. assurance, balance, composure, control, dignity.

poison N. toxin, venom, virus, contagion.

poisonous ADJ. venomous, toxic, fatal, deadly, noxious.

poke V. shove, push, jab, thrust.

polish V. rub, shine, brighten, gloss.

polite ADJ. courteous, refined, civil, tactful, thoughtful.

pollute V. taint, contaminate, dirty, poison, defile.

pollution N. impurity, contamination, smog, dirt.

pompous ADJ. vain, arrogant, pretentious, inflated, egotistical.

ponder V. reflect, think, mediate, contemplate.

ponderous ADJ. boring, dreary, dull, cumbersome, massive, weighty.

poor ADJ. impoverished, destitute, broke, needy, meager, pitiful.

• **popular** ADJ. admired, liked, prevalent, current, favorite, public. *Kennedy was one of our most admired leaders.*

portion N. share, allotment, part, division, serving.

portray V. show, represent, depict, impersonate, describe.

pose V. sit, model, impersonate, masquerade, feign, pretend, put forth, ask.

• **position** N. location, site, posture, attitude, status, bearing. *Tell us your location on the mountain so we can send help.*

positive ADJ. decided, sure, definite, affirmative, certain, absolute.

positively ADV. absolutely, certainly, really, surely.

• **possess** V. own, bear, have, hold, control. *Few faculty members own an automobile.*

possession N. title, ownership, custody, property.

possessive ADJ. jealous, dominating, controlling.

- **possible** ADJ. feasible, practical, achievable, likely, potential. *The plan may prove feasible.*

post N. position, job; pole, column.

posture N. carriage, attitude, stance, condition.

potent ADJ. strong, effective, forceful, powerful, intense.

pour V. flow, swarm, flood, drench, decant.

poverty N. distress, destitution, dearth, want, starvation.

power N. strength, might, capacity, force, energy, efficacy.

powerful ADJ. mighty, strong, forceful, potent, dynamic, effective.

- **practical** ADJ. useful, handy, pragmatic, realistic, implicit. *We need useful ideas, not vague theories.*

practice N. rehearsal, repetition, exercise, tradition, custom.

praise N. commendation, esteem, tribute, appreciation, homage; —V. glorify, exalt, honor, compliment.

prank N. trick, joke, caper, antic.

prate N., V. chatter, babble.

pray V. appeal, entreat, supplicate, beg.

prayer N. supplication, appeal, invocation, request.

preacher N. cleric, clergyman, reverend (with *the*), minister, parson, priest.

precise ADJ. exact, meticulous, rigid, accurate, definite.

- **precisely** ADV. exactly, directly, specifically. *He will join us in exactly one hour.*

predicament N. dilemma, trouble, bind, emergency, pinch.

predict V. forecast, declare, foresee, anticipate, prophesy.

prediction N. forecast, projection, outlook, prophecy, warning.

predisposition N. taste, preference, bent, attitude.

preference N. favorite, choice, selection.

pregnant ADJ. expecting, with child, suggestive, meaningful, significant.

prejudice N. bias, intolerance, bigotry, antipathy, partiality.

preliminary ADJ. introductory, basic, primary, elemental, elementary.

prelude N. introduction, preface.

preoccupied ADJ. engrossed, absentminded, distracted, absorbed, oblivious, inattentive.

preparation N. arrangement, planning, readiness, preparedness.

prepare V. plan, arrange, ready, make, fix.

preponderance N. weight, dominance, abundance.

preposterous ADJ. extravagant, ridiculous, unreasonable, foolish, absurd.

prerogative N. privilege, right, authority, liberty, claim.

presence N. occurrence, attendance, vicinity, nearness.

present ADJ. current, existing, attending, here; — V. donate, give, introduce, exhibit, offer.

presentation N. introduction, gift, exhibition, speech.

preserve V. maintain, keep, save, protect, conserve.

press V. push, compress, finish; iron; insist, urge.

pressure N. tension, stress, force.

presume V. assume, suppose, guess, believe.

presumption N. assumption, supposition, arrogance, guess.

• **pretend** V. imagine, feign, simulate, fake, falsify. *The children liked to imagine they lived in a magic forest.*

pretense N. fraud, sham, charade, deception, air, facade.

pretext N. facade, excuse, guise, pretense.

prevailing ADJ. widespread, current, popular, general, predominant, common.

prevalent ADJ. general, widespread, comprehensive, prevailing, rife.

prevent V. deter, avert, interrupt, block, hinder, stop.

prevention N. deterrence, forestalling, circumvention, preclusion, hindrance.

• **previous** ADJ. former, prior, aforementioned, earlier, past. *Her former teacher plays in the symphony orchestra.*

prick V. stab, puncture, perforate, sting.

pride N. ego, confidence, assuredness, arrogance, self-esteem, vanity, conceit, satisfaction, fulfillment.

- **primary** ADJ. main, first, paramount, capital, key, initial. *Our main interest is in the welfare of our elders.*

primitive ADJ. early, primeval, uncivilized, simple, rough.

principal ADJ. foremost, primary, chief, first, leading, essential.

print V. publish, issue, letter.

printing N. publication, lettering, impression.

prior ADJ. previous, earlier, preceding, past.

private ADJ. confidential, personal, secret, concealed.

prize N. award, reward, trophy, treasure.

- **probable** ADJ. likely, possible, conceivable, presumable. *Two developments seem likely.*

probe V. explore, investigate, feel, inquire.

problem N. dilemma, predicament, riddle, difficulty.

proceed V. continue, go, progress, come.

proclamation N. declaration, announcement, broadcast, revelation.

prod V. encourage, push, urge.

prodigal ADJ. profuse, extravagant, wasteful.

prodigious ADJ. giant, fabulous, marvelous, talented.

produce V. make, spawn, bear, create, originate, manufacture.

product N. outcome, result, goods, merchandise, yield.

production N. manufacturing, creation, composition.

productive ADJ. efficient, creative, effective, fertile.

profane ADJ. obscene, temporal, secular, worldly, vulgar.

proficient ADJ. skilled, adept, competent, efficient, able.

profit N. benefit, improvement, earnings, advantage.

profitable ADJ. gainful, desirable, moneymaking, lucrative.

profound ADJ. abysmal, deep, learned, great, philosophical, serious, fathomless.

profuse ADJ. excessive, abundant, plentiful, opulent, thick.

program N. schedule, calendar, agenda, syllabus.

progress N. development, growth, advancement, progression, movement, increase.

progressive ADJ. broad, liberal, open-minded, advanced.

• **project** N. venture, enterprise, undertaking, design. *Broad public support will be required for the success of the venture.*

projection N. extension, outline, design, bulge, prominence, protuberance.

prolific ADJ. fertile, productive, teeming, propagating.

prolonged ADJ. sustained, continued, lengthened, stretched, chronic.

promise V. pledge, vow, guarantee, assure, swear.

promote V. encourage, publicize, advertise, elevate, advance, upgrade.

pronounce V. utter, speak, vocalize, proclaim, announce.

proof N. testimony, evidence, reason, confirmation.

propel V. move, thrust, urge, shoot, drive.

prophet N. clairvoyant, oracle, seer, fortune-teller.

prophetic ADJ. oracular, sybilline.

proportion N. share, piece, section, balance, comparison, symmetry.

proposal N. suggestion, proposition, offer, plan.

propose V. suggest, offer, pose, state.

prosaic ADJ. ordinary, common, dull, everyday.

prosecute V. sue, wage, perform, try.

prosper V. thrive, flourish, succeed.

prosperity N. success, welfare, comfort, ease, opulence, affluence.

protective ADJ. preventive, careful, preservative.

prototype N. original, model, ancestor.

proud ADJ. confident, arrogant, vain, egotistical, conceited, self-assured, dignified, honorable, high-minded.

prove V. demonstrate, show, verify, justify, corroborate.

proverb N. maxim, adage, saying, aphorism, byword.

• **provide** V. supply, offer, give, bestow. *The company will supply materials for the display.*

province N. area, department, domain, district.

provision N. condition, arrangement, stipulation, specification.

provoke V. incite, anger, taunt, annoy, irritate.

prudence N. discretion, restraint, caution, economy, foresight.

prudent ADJ. cautious, sane, wary, economical, wise, sensible.

psychology N. mind, psyche, mentality, ethos.

public ADJ. civil, popular, open, national, civic; — N. people, society, community.

publish V. print, issue, reveal, publicize, announce.

pull V. tug, draw, pluck, drag, haul, tow.

punch V. kick, hit, drive, pound.

punctual ADJ. exact, timely, prompt, on time.

pungent ADJ. acid, biting, sharp, strong.

punish V. correct, discipline, scold, imprison, chastise.

punishment N. discipline, correction, punition.

purchase V. obtain, buy, acquire.

pure ADJ. genuine, authentic, unadulterated, absolute, perfect.

purge V. purify, cleanse, clear, eliminate.

purification N. disinfection, cleansing, catharsis, purgation.

purify V. clear, wash, cleanse, refine, clarify.

purity N. chastity, cleanliness, clarity, virginity.

purport N. significance, meaning, idea, tendency, trend.

• **purpose** N. function, objective, intention, aim, goal. *The function of this gear is to drive the flywheel.*

pursue V. chase, follow, seek, hunt.

pursuit N. chase, search, quest, vocation, occupation, business.

push V. shove, force, propel, elbow, encourage, drive.

put V. deposit, set, place, lay, install, position.

putrid ADJ. rotten, moldy, bad, decayed.

puzzle N. question, mystery, problem, riddle.

Q

quaint ADJ. unusual, strange, curious, funny.

quake V. tremble, shake, shudder, vibrate.

qualification N. eligibility, fitness, provision.

qualified ADJ. capable, adequate, experienced, able.

- **qualify** V. limit, suit, fit, restrict, distinguish. *Let me limit my comments by confining them to recent legislation.*

- **quality** N. grade, class, caliber, condition, characteristic, feature, attribute. *We tried to purchase the best grade of lumber.*

quantity N. amount, measure, bulk, total, whole.

quantum N. quantity, allotment, amount.

quarrelsome ADJ. irritable, argumentative, belligerent, unruly, petulant.

quarter N. neighborhood, area, section.

queer ADJ. unique, extraordinary, eccentric, unusual, curious, fantastic.

quench V. repress, extinguish, crush, destroy.

quest N. pursuit, journey, search, inquiry, expedition.

- **question** N. inquiry, problem, doubt, uncertainty; —V. ask, interrogate, doubt. *Send your inquiry to the appropriate office.*

questionable ADJ. debatable, uncertain, doubtful, enigmatic, ambiguous.

questioning ADJ. incredulous, curious, doubtful, uncertain.

quick ADJ. fast, hurried, brief, speedy, rapid, instantaneous.

quicken V. enliven, animate, speed up, energize.

quickness N. speed, facility, sharpness, agility.

quiet ADJ. serene, still, calm, peaceful, silent, tranquil.

quintessence N. basis, nature, essence, heart.

quintessential ADJ. essential, basic, typical.

quit V. leave, abandon, resign, retire, relinquish.

quite ADV. somewhat, completely, rather, entirely, considerably.

quiz N. examination, puzzle, test, riddle.

quotidian ADJ. daily, regular, everyday.

R

race N. competition, contest, match, breed, nation, people, tribe; —V. compete, run, hurry, dash.

radiate V. shed, gleam, diffuse, spread.

radical ADJ. primary, original, intrinsic, basic, extreme, violent.

rage N. fury, anger, enthusiasm, wrath.

raid V. assault, invade, attack, steal.

raise V. increase, boost, lift, produce, cultivate.

rally V. assemble, meet, concentrate, mobilize.

ram V. push, drive, stab, cram, crowd.

random ADJ. irregular, haphazard, indiscriminate, accidental, purposeless.

range N. scope, area, extent, limit, territory; —V. roam, wander, change, arrange, go.

rank N. order, class, degree, level.

rant V. fume, rave.

rape V. assault, violate, force.

rare ADJ. scarce, uncommon, infrequent, unique, extraordinary.

rash ADJ. foolhardy, thoughtless, precipitate, hasty, impulsive.

rate N. velocity, speed, ratio, proportion; —V. estimate, class.

rational ADJ. sane, reasonable, logical, sensible, normal.

rationalize V. justify, account for.

rattle V. shake, clatter, clack; embarrass, confuse, fluster.

rave V. rant, fume, rage, storm.

ravenous ADJ. ferocious, insatiable, greedy, voracious.

raw ADJ. green, crude, uncooked, rude, obscene.

reach V. attain, achieve, get, accomplish.

reactionary ADJ. royalist, unprogressive, ultraconservative, fanatic.

read V. browse, study, understand, perceive, foresee, indicate.

readiness N. preparation, ease, dexterity.

• **ready** ADJ. prepared, equipped, willing, suitable, disposed. *They were prepared for a long siege.*

real ADJ. authentic, tangible, actual, genuine.

realistic ADJ. natural, lifelike, objective, pragmatic.

• **reality** N. actuality, verity, truth, existence. *In actuality, few miners fell ill from the gas leak.*

realize V. accomplish, actualize, carry out, recognize, understand.

• **really** ADV. actually, positively, indeed, absolutely, honestly. *The clown is actually a famous actress in disguise.*

rear N. bottom, back, rump, tail.

reason N. motive, ground, purpose, argument, understanding, intelligence, sanity; —V. justify, conclude, argue.

reasonable ADJ. rational, sensible, logical, sane.

rebel V. overthrow, revolt, rise up.

rebellion N. revolution, mutiny, insurrection, upheaval, riot.

rebirth N. revival, conversion, renaissance.

recall V. remember, recollect, reminisce, annul, revoke.

recede V. retreat, withdraw, wane, regress, ebb.

• **receive** V. get, acquire, obtain. *They frequently get compliments on their ability to work together as a team.*

receptive ADJ. open-minded, accepting, responsive, sensory, open.

reciprocate V. return, give back, retaliate, requite.

reckless ADJ. foolhardy, rash, careless, wild, irresponsible.

reckon V. estimate, suppose, regard, count.

reckoning N. calculation, estimation, count, account.

reclaim V. save, redeem, restore, renovate.

recline V. rest, lie, relax.

recognition N. credit, acknowledgment, recollection.

• **recognize** V. know, recall, acknowledge, perceive, accept. *Do you know all of the guests by first name?*

recoil V. reflect, bounce, rebound, react, echo.

recollection N. remembrance, memory.

recommendation N. reference, advice, praise, approval, suggestion.

recompense V. pay, compensate.

reconcile V. reunite, conciliate, settle, harmonize, mediate.

reconciliation N. rectification, conciliation, rapprochement.

recondition V. restore, rebuild, renew, overhaul.

reconsider V. review, rethink, reevaluate.

reconstruct V. remold, repair, rejuvenate, put together again.

record N. document, schedule, history, chronicle, report; —V. transcribe, register, enter, log.

recover V. redeem, retrieve, reclaim, mend, improve, recuperate.

recovery N. recuperation, comeback, retrieval.

recreation N. amusement, relaxation, play, pastime, game.

rectify V. correct, fix, remedy, improve, adjust.

recur V. reappear, return, revive.

recurrent ADJ. chronic, seasonable, periodic, cyclic.

redeem V. liberate, free, rescue, compensate, atone.

redress V. remedy, amend, restore, repair, compensate.

reduce V. curtail, lower, lessen, decrease.

reduction N. decrease, cutback, demotion.

redundant ADJ. wordy, verbose, repetitious, superfluous.

refer V. mention, allude, specify, attribute, cite.

reference N. recommendation, testimonial, allusion, citation.

refine V. purify, perfect, clean, clarify.

refined ADJ. cultured, delicate, elegant, purified.

reflect V. contemplate, think, reason, consider.

reflection N. thought, study, echo, image.

refrain V. withhold, keep, abstain, inhibit, restrain.

refresh V. restore, renew, energize, awaken, animate.

refusal N. rejection, denial, decline, turndown.

register V. catalog, record, list, enter, enroll.

regret V. lament, sorrow, rue, repent, deplore; — N. rue, repentance, grievance.

• **regular** ADJ. ordinary, steady, uniform, customary. *The military will follow ordinary procedures in acquiring new weaponry.*

reiterate V. repeat, restate, reinforce.

rejection N. refusal, denial, exclusion, dismissal, elimination.

rejoice V. celebrate, delight, exalt, revel.

rejuvenate V. refresh, restore, modernize, renew.

relapse V. regress, blackslide, retrogress, revert, lapse.

relate V. narrate, recount, describe, report, tell.

related ADJ. kindred, akin, associated, allied.

relation N. association, connection, link, similarity.

• **relative** N. relation, family, kin; —ADJ. conditional, dependent, relevant, pertinent. *He willed the property to a relation.*

relax V. rest, recline, ease, unwind, loosen.

release V. liberate, free, emancipate, discharge, announce, emit.

relent V. weaken, soften, subside, relax, abate.

relentless ADJ. rigorous, hard, strict, unyielding, stubborn, continual.

relevant ADJ. pertinent, applicable, appropriate, germane.

reliable ADJ. dependable, trustworthy.

relic N. trace, fossil, ruin.

relief N. assistance, help, support, comfort, deliverance.

relieve V. comfort, aid, help, console, appease.

religious ADJ. devout, holy, spiritual, pious, reverent.

relinquish V. forego, abandon, renounce, reject, abdicate.

relish V. appreciate, enjoy, prefer, admire.

remain V. wait, continue, endure.

remainder N. surplus, balance, remains, rest.

remark N. comment, observation, statement; — V. mention, comment, observe.

- **remarkable** ADJ. extraordinary, unusual, rare, striking. *We witnessed an extraordinary feat of strength.*

remedial ADJ. curative, corrective.

remedy N. medicine, cure, antidote, counteraction.

remember V. recall, reminisce, retrace, recollect, think of.

remit V. forgive, pardon, release, absolve, alleviate.

remnant N. residue, surplus, remainder, relic, ruin.

remorseful ADJ. repentant, penitential, contrite, sorry, regretful.

remote ADJ. separate, distant, obscure, isolated, slender, negligible.

remove V. eliminate, withdraw, take out, annihilate, transport, dislodge, move.

render V. return, abdicate, give, pay, express, communicate.

rendezvous N. meeting, engagement, date, appointment.

renew V. restore, refresh, renovate, recondition, continue, extend.

renovate V. remodel, renew, modernize, repair.

renown N. fame, eminence, distinction, reputation.

repay V. compensate, return, avenge.

repeal V. lift, abolish, cancel, end, reverse.

repeat V. restate, reiterate, echo, recapitulate, recite.

repel V. rebuff, parry, repulse, reject, disgust.

repetition N. reiteration, echo, restatement.

repetitive ADJ. reiterative, repetitious.

replace V. substitute, restore, reconstruct, reinstate, supplant, supersede.

report N. record, account, story, description, news, announcement.

represent V. describe, delineate, depict, illustrate, epitomize, personify, embody.

repress V. silence, suppress, quell, subdue.

reproduce V. multiply, breed, proliferate, copy.

repudiate V. disclaim, deny, forsake, abandon, banish, expel.

repulse V. disgust, offend, nauseate, repel.

reputation N. name, character, honor, repute.

repute V. think, suppose, believe, report.

request V. appeal, entreat, ask, solicit.

require V. demand, expect, mandate, suppose.

requirement N. demand, mandate, exigency, claim, need, necessity, condition.

requite V. compensate, reciprocate, reward, pay, retaliate, avenge.

rescind V. revoke, annul, veto, cancel, abolish.

rescue V. free, save, liberate, release, recover, salvage.

resemble V. agree, correspond, take after, favor.

reserve V. hold, save, keep, maintain.

resign V. leave, quit, abandon, surrender, renounce, abdicate.

resist V. obstruct, contest, withstand, combat, oppose.

resistance N. insusceptibility, immunity, opposition, refusal.

resistant ADJ. impervious, immune, resistive.

resolute ADJ. constant, determined, faithful, decisive, steadfast, firm.

resolution N. decision, resolve, determination, courage, devotion.

resolve V. settle, decide, unravel, solve, determine.

resonant ADJ. sonorous, mellow, resounding, vibrant.

resort N. refuge, expedient; —V. turn, refer, use.

resourceful ADJ. inventive, creative, ingenious, fertile.

respect N. admiration, esteem, reverence, honor; —V. admire, revere, esteem.

respectable ADJ. honorable, decent, acceptable, upright, good.

respite N. pause, break.

respond V. reply, react, acknowledge.

response N. answer, reaction, acknowledgment, reply.

responsive ADJ. receptive, approachable, sensitive.

restate V. repeat, paraphrase.

restless ADJ. uneasy, nervous, jumpy, anxious, worried.

restore V. renew, reinstate, replace, mend, repair, revamp, reestablish, reinstall.

restrain V. check, control, inhibit, bridle, hold.

restricted ADJ. limited, fixed, local, confidential.

result N. conclusion, outcome, consequence, effect, answer.

resume V. continue, recommence, reoccupy, reclaim.

retain V. hold, keep, maintain, preserve, employ.

retaliation N. retribution, vengeance, reciprocation, counterattack.

retard V. delay, hinder, hamper, interrupt, slow.

retinue N. following, entourage, train.

retire V. withdraw, leave, step down, retreat.

retirement N. seclusion, retreat, withdrawal.

retort V. answer, respond, comeback, reply.

retract V. disavow, withdraw, revoke, abjure, recall.

retreat V. withdraw, pull back, depart, leave, recede.

retrograde V. deteriorate, recede, retrogress, backslide, degenerate.

return V. restore, revert, recur, earn, draw, yield.

revamp V. modernize, fix, rebuild, revise.

reveal V. expose, divulge, unveil, uncover, disclose, show.

revelation N. disclosure, unveiling, exposé, apocalypse.

revenge N. retaliation, vengeance, retribution, vindictiveness.

reverence N. honor, respect, adoration, homage, esteem.

reverie N. dream, daydream, trance.

reverse V. repeal, annul, retract; invert, turn around, shift, transfer; —ADJ. opposite, transposed.

• **review** V. critique, judge, examine, analyze, rehearse, inspect; —N. critique, commentary, examination. *The author disliked the biting critique of her play.*

revise V. amend, rework, alter, update, improve.

revision N. improvement, alteration, amendment, reworking.

revival N. reawakening, resurrection, renewal, rebirth, rejuvenation.

revive V. reawaken, revitalize, arouse, rejuvenate, restore, remember.

revoke V. lift, repeal, reverse, overturn, annul.

revolution N. upheaval, cataclysm, rebellion, overthrow, uprising.

revolve V. rotate, turn, spin, circle.

reward N. recompense, award, prize, dividend, bounty.

rhetorical ADJ. sonorous, oratorical.

rhythm N. cadence, beat, meter, pulsation, measure.

rich ADJ. opulent, abundant, wealthy, affluent, luxurious.

riches N. treasure, fortune, wealth, worth.

rid V. free, eliminate, clear, release, shed, exterminate.

ride V. drive, journey, go, drift.

ridicule V. mock, satirize, deride, mimic, caricature.

right ADJ. correct, appropriate, true, proper, lawful, honest.

righteous ADJ. honest, ethical, moral, upstanding.

rigid ADJ. unbending, inflexible, stiff, stubborn, severe.

rigor N. severity, difficulty, oppression, inflexibility.

ring N. loop, circle, band, gang, confederation, league.

riot N. disturbance, rebellion, uprising, tumult, insurgence.

riotous ADJ. violent, disorderly, profuse.

rise V. scale, climb, ascend, mount, increase, heighten, escalate, succeed.

risk N. chance, danger, hazard, gamble, adventure.

ritual N. ceremony, formality, sacrament, observance, service.

rival N. competitor, adversary, opponent, challenger; —V. challenge, oppose, dispute, confront, contest.

roar V. cry, yell, shout, call, scream.

rob V. steal, burglarize, plunder, thieve, deprive.

rock V. shake, toss, disturb, agitate.

roll V. tumble, rotate, turn, revolve.

romantic ADJ. idealistic, sentimental, poetic, fanciful, imaginary, beautiful, amorous.

room N. margin, space, leeway; chamber.

root N. basis, cause, origin, heart, center.

rotate V. revolve, turn, spin, alternate.

rotation N. interchange, alternation, revolution, circulation.

rotten ADJ. filthy, bad, degenerate, spoiled, putrid, decayed.

rough ADJ. coarse, jagged, uneven, harsh, abrasive, impolite, violent, agitated, unfinished, preliminary, tentative.

round ADJ. spherical, circular, orbed, globular.

routine N. method, system, way, habit; —ADJ. customary, habitual.

row N. quarrel, disturbance, argument; file, line, series.

rubric N. rule, prescript, regulation, law.

rude ADJ. vulgar, insolent, uncouth, disrespectful, impolite.

rueful ADJ. sorrowful, melancholy, regretful, plaintive, depressed, sad.

rugged ADJ. rough, hard, difficult, harsh, arduous.

ruin V. destroy, spoil, wreck, break, demolish; —
N. devastation, destruction, downfall, undoing;
relic, wreckage, remnant.

rule N. law, regulation, prescript, rubric.

ruling N. pronouncement, decree, edict; —ADJ.
dominant, supreme, prevailing.

rumble V. thunder, roar, growl, boom.

run V. sprint, dash, bolt, hurry, hasten; work,
operate, function.

rupture N. breech, breakage, crack.

rush V. hasten, hurry, speed, hustle, dash.

rustic ADJ. natural, unpolished, pastoral, rural,
unadorned.

S

sabotage V. undermine, impair, subvert, disable.

sacred ADJ. hallowed, blessed, holy, divine, consecrated.

sacrifice N. offering, libation, abnegation, atonement, cost.

sacrilege N. profanity, irreverence, blasphemy, desecration, impiousness.

sad ADJ. gloomy, sorrowful, unhappy, depressing, melancholy.

saddened ADJ. depressed, sorrowed, dejected, dismayed.

sadness N. gloom, sorrow, unhappiness, dejection, melancholy, woe.

safe ADJ. secure, sheltered, protected, guarded, unhurt, unharmed.

safety N. preservation, assurance, security, escape.

sag V. droop, sink, wilt, slip.

sage ADJ. rational, wise, logical, experienced; — N. intellectual, savant, scholar.

sail V. rush, flow, fly.

salutation N. greeting, welcoming, hello.

salvage V. save, recover, rescue.

same ADJ. identical, equal, consistent, equivalent.

sample N. specimen, model, example, case, illustration.

sanction N. penalty, approbation, approval,

privilege, authorization; —V. support,
encourage, authorize.

sanctity N. sacredness, holiness, inviolability.

sane ADJ. sensible, rational, reasonable, prudent,
lucid, levelheaded.

sanity N. reason, sense, saneness, lucidity, sound
mind.

sarcasm N. irony, scorn, bitterness, causticity,
hostility.

sarcastic ADJ. satirical, ironic, bitter, derisive,
scornful.

satiate V. satisfy, fulfill, gratify, gorge.

satire N. sarcasm, humor, irony, ridicule,
lampoon.

• **satisfactory** ADJ. acceptable, sufficient, adequate,
convincing. *The changes you recommend are
acceptable to the committee.*

satisfy V. fulfill, please, gratify, placate, content.

saturate V. drench, soak, permeate, wet, charge.

savage ADJ. uncivilized, crude, wild, fierce, cruel.

save V. store, collect, conserve, accumulate,
redeem.

savor V. enjoy, appreciate, feel.

say V. communicate, tell, express, articulate,
assert, claim.

saying N. proverb, maxim, adage, quotation,
byword.

scale V. climb, ascend, mount, grapple; —N.
ratio, gradation, balance, proportion.

scan V. skim, inspect, examine, browse, glance at.

scandalous ADJ. disreputable, shameful, outrageous, disgraceful, dishonorable.

scarce ADJ. rare, insufficient, infrequent, uncommon.

scare V. shock, frighten, startle, terrify, intimidate.

scary ADJ. frightening, startling, alarming, terrifying, fearful.

scatter V. disperse, sprinkle, spread, dispel.

scene N. setting, locale, site, view, area.

scent N. odor, smell, aroma, fragrance.

- **schedule** N. program, plan, timetable, list. *Be sure to make time in your program for the treasurer's report.*

scheme N., V. plot, design, plan, intrigue.

scholar N. student, intellectual, savant, researcher.

scholastic ADJ. pedagogic, learned, pedantic.

scold V. punish, reprimand, berate, reprove.

scorch V. burn, char, singe.

score N. tally, record, rating; —V. grade, mark, accomplish.

scour V. clean, scrub, scrape, forage, comb, seek, search.

scout V. search, explore, seek; —N. explorer, lookout.

scowl V. frown, glare, glower.

scramble V. blend, combine, shuffle, confuse.

scrape V. scrub, grate, scratch.

scratch V. scrape, mark, grate, nick.

scream N., V. wail, cry, howl, shriek, yell.

screech N., V. yell, cry, scream, shriek.

screen V. censor, shade, separate, protect, shield.

scrub V. scour, wash, clean, scrape.

scrutiny N. study, examination, inspection, investigation, search.

search V. examine, inspect, scrutinize, investigate, scour.

seat N. chair, bottom, center, base.

secluded ADJ. isolated, solitary, private, withdrawn, remote, hidden.

seclusion N. retirement, separation, hiding, isolation, withdrawal.

secondary ADJ. subordinate, minor, derivative.

secrecy N. privacy, seclusion, concealment, mystery.

secret ADJ. hidden, restricted, classified, confidential, private, unknown.

secretly ADV. covertly, clandestinely, furtively.

sect N. group, faction, religion, faith.

section N. division, part, segment, share, slice.

secure ADJ. fastened, tight, stable; sure, safe, confident; —V. tighten, fasten, acquire, obtain, protect.

seduce V. entice, tempt, allure, bait, coax.

seduction N. lure, debauchery.

seductive ADJ. enticing, alluring, tempting, inviting, bewitching.

see V. view, observe, regard, perceive, look, comprehend, understand, ascertain, determine.

seed N. pit, kernel, germ, spore; children, offspring.

seek V. search, quest, attempt, look for.

seem V. look, appear.

segment N. division, part, section, portion, cut.

segregate V. isolate, separate, ostracize.

seize V. confiscate, grab, capture, arrest, catch, take.

seldom ADV. infrequently, rarely, scarcely.

select V. pick, choose, elect; —ADJ. preferred, elite, best.

selection N. choice, preference, pick.

selective ADJ. discriminating, choosy.

self N. ego, character, personality, person.

self-assured ADJ. confident, proud.

self-confident ADJ. confident, assured, bold.

self-control N. reserve, restraint, caution, demure.

self-esteem N. pride, self-respect, reserve.

self-important ADJ. pompous, egocentric, conceited.

selfish ADJ. greedy, self-centered, stingy.

selfless ADJ. altruistic, kind, generous, unselfish.

self-respect N. pride, self-esteem.

self-restraint N. reserve, self-control.

self-sufficient N. independent, self-supporting.

sell V. market, trade, retail, peddle.

semblance N. shade, facade.

seminar N. meeting, class, conference, grouping.

send V. ship, forward, dispatch, mail.

senile ADJ. aged, doddering, weak, feeble, infirm.

senior ADJ. superior, advanced, higher, older, elder; —N. elder, superior, chief.

sensation N. feeling, perception, sense, response, wonder, marvel.

sensational ADJ. marvelous, dramatic, wonderful, thrilling, spectacular.

sense V. perceive, feel; —N. sanity, intelligence, reason, logic.

senseless ADJ. useless, unreasonable, mindless.

sensibility N. sensation, feeling, sense, insight.

sensible ADJ. reasonable, logical, rational, responsible, sane.

• **sensitive** ADJ. tender, delicate, emotional, susceptible. *The photographs touched our most tender emotions.*

sensitivity N. sensitiveness, sensation, tenderness.

sensual ADJ. carnal, earthy, material, physical, suggestive, sexual.

sensuous ADJ. sensual, voluptuous, epicurean.

sentiment N. feeling, emotion, belief, attitude.

sentimental ADJ. emotional, romantic, tender, maudlin.

separate V. divide, isolate, sever, detach; —ADJ. divergent, distinct, unique, individual.

separately ADV. apart, discretely.

separation N. division, distinction, isolation, segregation.

sequence N. series, order, arrangement, succession.

serene ADJ. tranquil, calm, peaceful, quiet.

series N. chain, succession, run, order.

serious ADJ. earnest, solemn, sober, pensive, grave, important.

serve V. wait on, attend, aid, help, do.

service N. duty, ceremony, favor, observance.

set N. collection, group, series, class; —V. lay, place, settle, establish, appoint, solidify.

setback N. hindrance, obstacle, problem.

settle V. establish, decide, conclude, arrange.

• **several** ADJ. some, many, a few, various. *Some autograph seekers waited by the stage door.*

severe ADJ. rigid, firm, hard, powerful, difficult, cruel.

severity N. harshness, intensity, rigor, austerity.

sexual ADJ. erotic, sensual, reproductive.

sexy ADJ. erotic, sensual, desirable.

shade N. dusk, shadow, darkness, penumbra, hue, tint, color.

shadow N. shade, darkness, dusk, image.

shaft N. hole, tunnel, stick, beam.

shake V. shiver, quake, tremble, rock, vibrate.

shallow ADJ. superficial, weak, shoal.

shame V. embarrass, dishonor; —N. humiliation, disgrace.

shameful ADJ. disgraceful, humiliating, dishonorable, embarrassing.

shameless ADJ. bold-faced, audacious, immodest, presumptuous, blatant.

shape N. figure, pattern, image, form, mold.

shapeless ADJ. amorphous, formless, unshaped, unformed.

share V. distribute, allot, contribute.

sharp ADJ. clear, acute, distinct, clever, intelligent.

shatter V. destroy, smash, break.

shave V. scrape, brush.

shed V. throw, cast, emit, project, molt.

shelter N. housing, sanctuary, haven, refuge; —V. hide, house, protect, shield.

shield V. defend, protect, guard, shelter, cover.

shift V. disturb, move, turn, change.

shine V. glow, radiate, glimmer, glare, irradiate.

shock V. startle, frighten, appall, alarm, horrify; —N. collision, jolt, impact.

shocking ADJ. outrageous, infamous, appalling, scandalous, terrible.

short ADJ. abrupt, brief, condensed, curt, sudden, little.

shortage N. lack, deficit, failure, scarcity, insufficience.

shorten V. edit, reduce, abridge, condense, shrink.

shout V. yell, cry, call, holler.

shove V. push, poke, drive, jostle.

show V. exhibit, display, demonstrate, divulge, unveil, indicate, guide.

shrill ADJ. piercing, high, sharp.

shrink V. contract, dwindle, diminish, wither, deflate.

sick ADJ. ill, unhealthy, morbid, impaired, ailing.

sickening ADJ. unspeakable, offensive, disgusting.

side N. part, flank, hand.

sign V. signal, gesture, endorse, autograph; —N. indication, symptom, gesture.

• **significance** N. importance, meaning, notability, prominence, weight. *We weighed the relative importance of the new developments.*

significant ADJ. important, expressive, meaningful, suggestive, critical, momentous.

signify V. emphasize, express; count, show, indicate, communicate, signal.

silence N. still, quiet, hush, soundlessness.

silent ADJ. still, quiet, hushed, tranquil, calm, speechless, noiseless, mute.

simple ADJ. plain, clear, easy, uncomplicated, natural.

simpleminded ADJ. slow, dumb, stupid, backward.

simplicity N. naiveté, modesty, informality.

simulate V. act, fake, copy, represent, imitate.

sin N. evil, corruption, crime, trespass.

sing V. chant, serenade, vocalize, hum.

single ADJ. sole, individual, unique, solitary, unmarried, free.

singular ADJ. exceptional, extraordinary, rare, unique, uncommon.

sink V. fall, drop, descend, submerge; —N. basin.

• **situation** N. circumstances, condition, position, location, place. *Welfare seemed the only alternative in his circumstances.*

size N. dimension, volume, expanse, magnitude, bulk.

skeptic N. doubter, pessimist, misanthrope, cynic, nihilist.

skeptical ADJ. doubtful, cynical, pessimistic, unbelieving, incredulous.

skill N. ability, proficience, mastery, training, dexterity.

skim V. brush, glance, graze, browse, scan.

skip V. overlook, disregard, omit, jump, hop, leap.

slam V. smash, bang, crash, wham.

slap V. hit, smack, slam, box.

sleep N., V. slumber, nap, doze, snooze.

sleepy ADJ. drowsy, somnolent, slumberous.

slide V. drift, glide, slip, coast, slither.

slip V. glide, err, slide, sag, blunder.

slippery ADJ. slick, shifty, evasive, sharp.

slope N. slant, inclination, incline, ascent.

slot N. position, place.

slow ADJ. gradual, unhurried, leisurely, delayed, boring, dull.

sluggishness N. laziness, slowness.

slumber N., V. sleep, rest, repose.

sly ADJ. shrewd, crafty, wily, cunning.

small ADJ. miniature, minute, little, minor, petty.

smart ADJ. intelligent, bright, wise, clever, keen.

smash V. destroy, break, crush, hit, demolish.

smear V. spread, cover, coat, wipe.

smell N. scent, aroma, odor, fragrance; —V. sniff, scent.

smile N., V. grin, beam.

smooth ADJ. even, flat, uniform, fluid, easy, effortless.

snap V. crack, break, click, clack.

snatch V. seize, catch, snare, grab.

sneak V. steal, creep, crawl, skulk.

snob N. elitist, sycophant.

soak V. wet, drench, immerse.

soar V. rise, fly, rocket, shoot.

sociable ADJ. friendly, gracious, social.

social ADJ. friendly, sociable, affable, outgoing, communicative.

socialize V. mingle, talk, nationalize, civilize.

• **society** N. public, civilization, community, nation. *Television programs must appeal to a broad segment of the public.*

soft ADJ. pliant, flexible, smooth, silky; compassionate, sensitive, gentle, quiet.

soften V. pacify, weaken, moderate.

soil V. stain, dirty, blacken, taint.

sole ADJ. single, alone, exclusive, only.

solid ADJ. firm, hard, sound, substantial, dense.

solitary ADJ. isolated, alone, lonely, deserted.

solitude N. isolation, detachment, removal, loneliness.

• **solution** N. answer, explanation, mixture. *The answer seemed simple once it was found.*

solve V. explain, resolve, decipher, unfold.

some ADJ. several, few.

sonorous ADJ. resonant, bombastic, rhetorical.

soothe V. comfort, calm, lull, quiet, pacify.

sophisticated ADJ. experienced, worldly, wise, cosmopolitan.

sordid ADJ. contemptible, ignoble, base, dirty.

sorrow N. grief, remorse, sadness, heartache, anguish.

sorrowful ADJ. mournful, grievous, sad, remorseful, distressed.

sorry ADJ. apologetic, regretful, remorseful.

sort V. arrange, separate, order; —N. variety, type, kind.

soul N. spirit, heart, being, essence, core.

sound N. noise; —ADJ. secure, stable, whole, unharmed, rational, sensible, cogent.

sour ADJ. tart, acerbic, tangy, sharp.

source N. origin, beginning, foundation, route, cause.

space N. room, area, expanse, distance.

spacious ADJ. broad, large, roomy.

span N. period, term, spread, extent.

spare V. save, economize, reserve; forgive, excuse.

spark V. flash, blink, light.

sparkle V. glisten, shine, flash, glimmer.

speak V. say, tell, talk, utter, articulate, communicate, express, converse.

speaker N. talker, presenter, spokesperson, orator.

special ADJ. distinctive, particular, exceptional, singular, individual.

• **specific** ADJ. particular, explicit, express, special, limited. *The panel wanted to examine particular aspects of the issue.*

specify V. name, designate, stipulate, define.

spectacular ADJ. staggering, amazing, dramatic, extraordinary.

speculate V. consider, think, surmise, suppose, gamble.

speech N. oration, lecture, address, talk, discourse.

speechless ADJ. mute, silent, wordless, dumb.

speed N. pace, velocity, rapidity, tempo, haste.

spend V. pay, give, disburse, consume, use.

spin V. rotate, turn, revolve, oscillate.

spirit N. vitality, enthusiasm, liveliness, animation, soul, psyche, animus, phantom, ghost.

spirited ADJ. excited, lively, vibrant, animated, fiery.

spiritless ADJ. dull, boring, languid, unenthusiastic.

spiritual ADJ. religious, immaterial, ecclesiastical, unworldly.

splash V. soak, douse, splatter, drench.

splendid ADJ. marvelous, superb, glorious, excellent, grand.

split V. break, cut, divide, crack.

spoil V. ruin, injure, damage, rot, decay.

spontaneous ADJ. distinctive, involuntary, automatic, compulsive.

sport N. game, recreation, play, athletics.

spot N. place, position, location; —N., V. stain, mark, blemish; —V. find, sight.

spread V. scatter, disperse, circulate, diffuse, strew.

spring N., V. jump, skip, bounce, leap.

sprinkle V. scatter, speckle, dust, spread.

squash V. smash, crush, suppress, crowd.

squeeze V. press, grip, crush, express, crowd.

stabilize V. balance, steady, solidify.

stagger V. wobble, sway, totter, reel, alternate, vary.

stain V. smear, discolor, tarnish, blot, soil.

stale ADJ. dry, flat, old, trite, old-fashioned.

stamp V. engrave, imprint, mark, crush, trample.

stand V. rise, endure, tolerate; —N. opinion, attitude.

• **standard** ADJ. common, accepted; —N. measure, mark, mean, model, average. *The house was built according to common construction practices.*

start V. begin, initiate, commence, launch; —N. commencement, beginning, onset.

startle V. frighten, shock, alarm, surprise, jolt.

startling ADJ. astounding, shocking, surprising, astonishing.

state N. nation, country, land, condition, situation; —V. assert, announce, declare, say, express.

statement N. assertion, announcement, declaration, account.

station N. base, post, depot; —V. put, place, position.

status N. condition, state, place, standing, rank.

stay V. continue, remain, rest, stop, hinder.

steadfast ADJ. fixed, faithful, stable.

steady ADJ. regular, even, steadfast, stable, solid, firm.

steal V. rob, take, burglarize, plunder.

steep ADJ. sheer, abrupt, sharp, towering.

steer V. drive, guide, maneuver, direct.

stem V. come, arrive, originate, hinder, stop.

step V. walk, come, move; —N. measure, action, stage.

sterile ADJ. unproductive, barren, infertile, impotent, boring.

sterilize V. fix, neuter, geld, castrate, sanitize, decontaminate, disinfect.

stick N. staff, cane, branch, twig; —V. puncture, stab, pierce.

stiff ADJ. firm, rigid, inflexible, hard, unyielding.

stifle V. muffle, smother, repress, censor.

still ADJ. quiet, motionless, peaceful, calm.

stimulate V. encourage, inspire, arouse, excite, animate.

stimulation N. encouragement, invigoration, arousal, excitement.

stimulus N. motivation, prod, catalyst, incitement.

sting V. prick, bite, irritate; —N. scam.

stir V. mix, agitate, arouse, inspire, stimulate.

stop V. cease, halt, discontinue, hinder, delay, obstruct.

store N. reserve, supply; market, shop; —V. keep, save, stockpile.

story N. narrative, tale, account, description.

stout ADJ. heavy, bulky, strong, fat, obese.

straight ADJ. direct, unswerving, unbent; honest, trustworthy, candid, frank.

straightforward ADJ. frank, direct, candid, honest, plain.

strain V. stress, harm, pull, injure, tighten, stretch.

strange ADJ. peculiar, odd, fantastic, bizarre, eccentric.

strength N. power, might, force, energy, muscle.

• **strengthen** V. reinforce, toughen, confirm, tighten. *It was necessary to reinforce the bridge pilings.*

strenuous ADJ. difficult, forceful, energetic, rough.

stress V. emphasize, underline, accentuate; —N. strain, pressure, importance, emphasis.

strict ADJ. severe, rigorous, harsh, stern, uncompromising.

stride V. stalk, march, stamp, stomp.

strike V. beat, hit, attack, affect; —N. protest, walkout.

striking ADJ. awesome, noticeable, shocking, impressive.

string N. line, series, run.

strive V. endeavor, labor, try, attempt.

stroll V. wander, amble, walk, saunter.

strong ADJ. powerful, mighty, forceful, resistant, solid, firm.

struggle V. battle, fight, contend, strive, clash.

stubborn ADJ. uncompromising, rigid, adamant, obstinate, relentless.

study V. consider, investigate, examine; —N. examination, research.

stumble V. lurch, blunder, trip, err.

stupefy V. perilize, daze, amaze.

stupendous ADJ. fabulous, amazing, marvelous, giant.

stupid ADJ. witless, inane, moronic, foolish, crass, asinine.

stupor N. daze, apathy, lethargy, torpor, inertness.

style N. mode, fashion, way, manner, tone.

suave ADJ. gallant, polite, gracious, courteous, tactful.

subject N. topic, theme, point, area, matter.

sublime ADJ. glorious, exalted, grand, magnificent.

submerge V. sink, submerse, flood, dip.

submit V. surrender, propose, yield, offer.

subordinate ADJ. lower, secondary, inferior, subservient.

subsequent ADJ. consecutive, following, future, later.

subservient ADJ. subordinate, servile, inferior, dependent.

subside V. ebb, abate, wane, moderate, slacken.

substance N. matter, body, import, material.

- **substantial** ADJ. large, heavy, considerable, sizable, important. *The performer balanced a large plate of fruit on his head.*

substantiate V. prove, concern, back.

substitute N. replacement, stand-in, alternate, surrogate.

subtle ADJ. indirect, fine, delicate.

succeed V. accomplish, triumph, prevail, achieve, surmount.

success N. prosperity, achievement, triumph, accomplishment.

succumb V. capitulate, bow, yield, fold, surrender.

suffer V. grieve, bear, endure, allow, tolerate.

suffering N. misery, agony, grief.

sufficient ADJ. adequate, plenty, enough, acceptable.

suggest V. imply, recommend, indicate, propose, hint.

- **suggestion** N. recommendation, hint, allusion, proposal, implication. *All of us are in favor of accepting your recommendation.*

suggestive ADJ. evocative, allusive, pregnant, insinuating, sensual.

suit V. become, satisfy, gratify, fit, conform, adapt; —N. litigation, prosecution.

suitable ADJ. becoming, fitting, eligible, appropriate.

summarize V. review, outline.

summary N. synopsis, résumé, recapitulation, abstract, outline; —ADJ. concise.

summation N. summary, total, addition.

summit N. peak, height, climax, top.

summon V. call, assemble, invoke.

super ADJ. marvelous, excellent, great.

superb ADJ. marvelous, extraordinary, magnificent, excellent, wonderful.

superficial ADJ. shallow, one-dimensional, surface, cursory, flimsy.

superfluous ADJ. excessive, unnecessary, useless, redundant, gratuitous.

• **superior** ADJ. greater, higher, better, excellent, supreme, sovereign. *Her daughter's achievement is certainly greater than her own.*

superiority N. arrogance, excellence, advantage.

supernatural ADJ. miraculous, transcendental, metaphysical, superhuman, divine, celestial.

supersede V. replace, take the place of, stand in for.

supervise V. overlook, administer, run, guide, conduct.

supple ADJ. limber, flexible, malleable, lithe.

supplement N. complement, addition, attachment, extension.

supply V. substitute, provide, give, furnish.

support V. maintain, keep, uphold, advocate, corroborate.

• **suppose** V. guess, presume, postulate, assume.
I guess his age to be well over fifty.

suppress V. overpower, crush, censor, quell, repress.

sure ADJ. certain, positive, strong, solid, definite.

surplus N. overage, excess, profusion, overabundance.

surprise V. astonish, shock, startle, amaze, stun.

surrender V. relinquish, succumb, abdicate, submit, collapse.

surround V. encompass, circle, confine, besiege, enclose.

survey V. overlook, examine, watch, scan.

survive V. persist, outlast, weather.

suspend V. discontinue, terminate, cease, interrupt.

suspicion N. doubt, distrust, feeling.

suspicious ADJ. doubtful, mistrustful, shady, distrustful.

sustain V. carry, support, bear, uphold, maintain.

sway V. wobble, teeter, bend; persuade, influence, affect.

swear V. curse, damn, blaspheme; declare, assert, vow.

sweet ADJ. adorable, attractive, sugary, pleasant, agreeable, nice, charming.

swift ADJ. fast, quick, speedy, rapid.

swing V. sway, pivot, oscillate, waver.

symbol N. emblem, character, representation, attribute.

symbolic ADJ. indicative, emblematic, representational.

symbolize V. represent, stand for.

symmetrical ADJ. regular, balanced, proportional, accordant, congruous.

sympathize V. empathize, understand, identify, feel.

sympathy N. pity, empathy, compassion, feeling, sentiment.

synopsis N. summary, abstract, brief, condensation.

synthetic ADJ. plastic, man-made, artificial, chemical.

system N. arrangement, plan, way, method, totality, whole, entity.

T

table N. inventory, chart, catalog; counter, desk.

taboo ADJ. forbidden, prohibited.

tacit ADJ. silent, implicit, implied, presupposed, accepted.

taciturn ADJ. reticent, reserved, silent, uncommunicative, laconic.

tack N. turn, approach.

tact N. diplomacy, savoir faire, judgment, subtlety, poise, acumen.

tactic N. move, maneuver, strategy, approach.

tactless ADJ. impolite, brash, rude, indelicate.

tail N. end, rear; —V. follow, watch, shadow.

taint V. corrupt, pollute, dirty, contaminate.

take V. seize, hold, capture, select, choose, bring, lead, buy, purchase, steal, remove.

tale N. anecdote, lie, story.

talent N. faculty, aptitude, gift, skill.

talk V. converse, speak, communicate, address, verbalize, articulate.

talkative ADJ. conversational, chatty, garrulous, glib.

tall ADJ. high, elevated, towering, big.

tally V. add, score, count.

tame ADJ. docile, domesticated, gentle, broken, boring, unexciting.

tamper V. meddle, fool, interfere, trouble, intervene.

tangible ADJ. tactile, palpable, physical, real.

tangle V. snarl, confuse, jumble, complicate; —N. maze, jungle, puzzle, quandary.

tantalize V. tease, bait, provoke, tempt, lure.

tap V. strike, pat, hit.

tardy ADJ. slow, late, overdue.

target N. aim, goal, mark, intention.

tarnish V. blacken, dirty, taint, stain, discolor.

tarry V. loiter, linger, remain, pause.

task N. duty, job, chore, effort.

taste V. savor, try, feel, experience.

tasteful ADJ. pleasing, aesthetic, delicious.

tasteless ADJ. flavorless, flat, insipid, bland.

tasty ADJ. tasteful, delicious, flavorful.

tattle V. blab, gossip, inform, reveal.

taunt V. bother, ridicule, tease, pester.

taut V. tight, close, snug, neat.

tax N. duty, tariff, levy, assessment.

teach V. educate, instruct, school, tutor, train.

teaching N. education, instruction, guidance, doctrine.

team N. group, crew, band, assembly.

tear V. rip, rupture, split, cleave.

tearful ADJ. weeping, crying, mournful, sobbing, lamenting.

tease V. tantalize, annoy, irritate, pester, bother.

technicality N. detail, specific.

• **technique** N. approach, method, system, way.
Your approach obviously requires great skill.

tedious ADJ. boring, wearisome, monotonous,
drowsy.

tedium N. monotony, boredom, fatigue.

teem V. bustle, overflow, swarm, abound.

teeter V. sway, wobble, lurch, totter.

telephone V. call, dial, buzz, ring, phone.

tell V. inform, explain, advise, relate, say.

temerity N. boldness, rashness, nerve, audacity,
indiscretion, daring.

temper N. fury, anger, passion, rage; mood,
spirit, disposition.

temperament N. disposition, mood, humor,
personality, character, nature.

temperamental ADJ. moody, capricious, irritable,
sensitive.

temperate ADJ. moderate, mild, frugal,
reasonable, abstinent.

tempestuous ADJ. stormy, turbulent, rough.

temporal ADJ. earthly, terrestrial, impermanent,
transitory.

• **temporary** ADJ. provisional, passing, momentary,
acting, interim, transitory. *The committee can give
only provisional approval to the request.*

tempt V. seduce, entice, allure, attract, invite.

tenable ADJ. justifiable, defensible, defendable.

tenacious ADJ. obstinate, tough, stubborn, persistent, sticky, resolute.

tend V. incline, lean, dispose; watch, guard, protect.

• **tendency** N. propensity, bent, thrust, predisposition, inclination. *She has a propensity for saying just the right thing at the right time.*

tender ADJ. loving, gentle, kind, compassionate, warm.

tense ADJ. stiff, rigid, taut, edgy, uptight.

• **tension** N. stress, pressure, strain, apprehension, fear. *Most of the engineers admitted to feeling stress during the strike.*

tentative ADJ. anticipated, indecisive, untested, temporary.

tenuous ADJ. insignificant, weak, insubstantial, implausible, feeble.

tenure N. occupancy, incumbency, occupation.

tepid ADJ. unenthusiastic, dull, lukewarm, halfhearted.

term N. interval, period, duration, span, expression, phrase, word.

terminal ADJ. concluding, last, final, ending; deadly, fatal.

terminate V. end, close, suspend, cease, dismiss.

terrain N. land, topography, territory.

• **terrific** ADJ. marvelous, excellent, extraordinary, horrible, ghastly. *The art exhibit was marvelous in its range and variety of paintings.*

territory N. terrain, area, country, region, section.

terror N. fear, panic, horror, dread, alarm.

terrorize V. frighten, abuse, bother.

test N. examination, proof, essay; —V. examine, inspect, try, assess, verify, experiment.

testify V. witness, attest, confirm, certify, state.

testimony N. confirmation, proof, affirmation, declaration, witness.

testy ADJ. irritable, ill-tempered, petulant, touchy.

text N. subject, passage, verse; manual, book.

texture N. grain, fiber, essence, feel, character, constitution.

thank V. oblige, bless.

thankful ADJ. obliged, grateful, appreciative.

thankless ADJ. ungrateful, critical, unappreciative, insensible.

thaw V. melt, dissolve, liquefy.

theatrical ADJ. dramatic, spectacular, showy, affected.

theft N. robbery, larceny, embezzlement, burglary, misappropriation.

thematic ADJ. topical.

theme N. topic, subject, composition, thesis.

theoretical ADJ. speculative, hypothetical, abstract.

theory N. hypothesis, premise, supposition, speculation, conjecture.

therapy N. treatment.

thesis N. dissertation, essay, theme, doctrine.

thick ADJ. solid, crowded, compact, heavy, dense, stupid.

thicken V. condense, solidify, compact.

thief N. robber, criminal, burglar, larcener.

thin ADJ. gaunt, slender, bony, lean, skinny.

thing N. object, being, entity, obsession, mania.

think V. contemplate, ponder, consider, meditate, feel, believe.

thirst N. craving, desire, appetite, longing.

thirsty ADJ. parched, dry, eager.

thorny ADJ. spiny, prickly, perplexing, complicated, difficult.

• **thorough** ADJ. careful, complete, accurate, entire, absolute. *The task was accomplished in a careful way.*

thought N. reflection, consideration, idea, meditation.

thoughtful ADJ. attentive, kind, pensive, museful, speculative.

thoughtless ADJ. careless, impulsive, inconsiderate, foolish.

thrash V. whip, beat, punish, defeat, flail.

thread N. filament, strand, fiber.

threat N. menace, warning, intimidation, danger.

threaten V. intimidate, menace, forewarn, impend.

thrift N. prudence, economy, frugality.

thrill N. excitement, shock, sensation.

thrive V. prosper, flourish, succeed, increase.

throb V. pulsate, palpitate, beat.

throe N. convulsion, pain, spasm, grip.

throttle V. repress, choke.

through ADJ. over, finished, completed, done; —ADV. completely, out; —PREP. past.

throw V. cast, toss, project, fling, pitch.

thrust V. push, shove, penetrate, pierce; —N. essence, substance, core.

thug N. hooligan, bully, gangster, punk, ruffian.

ticket N. marker, tag, label.

tickle V. delight, please, amuse.

ticklish ADJ. fragile, capricious, delicate.

tidy ADJ. neat, clean, orderly, trim.

tie V. bind, fasten, secure, attach, link.

tight ADJ. secure, taut, firm, sealed, locked, tense, arduous, difficult.

tight-lipped ADJ. taciturn, speechless.

till V. labor, work, plow, cultivate, sow.

tilt V. slant, lean, incline.

time N. interval, period, season, occasion, tempo, rhythm.

timeless ADJ. eternal, continual, everlasting, ageless.

timely ADJ. appropriate, opportune, convenient, proper, suitable.

timid ADJ. shy, fearful, cowardly, weak, modest.

tinge N., V. shade, tint, color.

tinker V. fiddle, putter, tamper.

tint N. color, tinge, hue, shade, tone.

tiny ADJ. small, miniature, diminutive, little.

tip N. end, peak, point; hint, clue.

tirade N. condemnation, abuse, denunciation, sermon, lecture.

tire V. exhaust, weaken, fatigue, bore.

tireless ADJ. active, enthusiastic, inexhaustible, energetic.

tiring ADJ. exhausting, boring, wearying, taxing, fatiguing.

title N. possession, ownership, claim, heading, name.

toast N. pledge, congratulations.

together ADV. simultaneously, concurrently, in unison.

toil V. labor, work, slave, drudge; —N. labor, grind, struggle.

token N. symbol, mark, sign, memorial, keepsake.

tolerable ADJ. bearable, allowable, acceptable.

tolerance N. leniency, charity, forbearance, consideration.

tolerant ADJ. patient, charitable, soft, lenient, merciful.

tolerate V. stand, permit, endure, suffer, allow, bear.

tone N. tint, color, intonation, accent, inflection.

tonic ADJ. refreshing, stimulating, energizing, invigorating.

tool N. instrument, utensil, implement, apparatus.

top N. summit, peak, pinnacle; —ADJ. maximum, excellent, uppermost, highest.

topple V. overturn, fall, surrender, overthrow.

torment V. annoy, provoke, torture, harass, bother.

torpor N. lethargy, inaction, sluggishness, apathy, indolence.

torrid ADJ. passionate, hot, sweltering, sultry.

tortuous ADJ. winding, indirect, curving.

torture N. anguish, torment, cruelty, persecution.

toss V. throw, fling, pitch, hurl, tumble, writhe.

total N. summation, aggregate, whole, sum, all; —ADJ. complete, absolute, entire.

tote V. carry, bear.

touch V. handle, feel, move, affect, contact; talent, ability.

touching ADJ. effective, moving, affecting, tender, emotional.

tough ADJ. difficult, hard, rough, severe, strong.

tour V. visit, travel; —N. voyage, trip, excursion, turn, circle.

tourist N. sightseer, visitor.

towering ADJ. overwhelming, outstanding, awesome, lofty.

toxic ADJ. lethal, poisonous, deadly, fatal.

toy N. plaything, game.

trace N. remnant, hint, suggestion, mark, sign.

track N. trace, print, trail; —V. follow.

tract N. area, lot, region, territory.

tractable ADJ. obedient, loyal, submissive, compliant.

trade N. business, dealings, commerce, exchange.

tradition N. lore, convention, heritage.

traffic N. business, commerce, patronage, trade.

tragedy N. misery, disaster, misfortune, accident.

trail V. draw, drag, track, follow, pursue.

train V. educate, prepare, teach, tutor.

trample V. stomp, tramp, squash, crush.

tranquil ADJ. calm, peaceful, undisturbed, quiet, still.

transcend V. surpass, go beyond.

transcendent ADJ. theoretical, ultimate, original, idealistic, visionary.

transfer V. give, seed, change, assign, move, shift.

transform V. revolutionize, change, convert, modify, remodel.

transgress V. breach, infringe, violate, offend, trespass.

transition N. passage, change, transformation, development.

transitory ADJ. temporary, momentary, fleeting, transient.

translate V. decipher, interpret, transform, convert.

transmit V. conduct, send, pass, communicate.

transparent ADJ. obvious, clear, evident, explicit, translucent, limpid.

transpire V. ooze, come, happen, come about.

transport V. carry, move, transfer, shift.

transportation N. transport, transit, carriage, conveyance.

trap N. ambush, snare, pitfall, ruse, lure.

trash N. garbage, waste, refuse, rubble, junk.

trauma N. shock, wound.

travel V. journey, roam, wander, go.

traverse V. cross, pass, cover, span.

travesty N. parody, caricature, ridicule, mockery.

treacherous ADJ. dangerous, unreliable, malevolent, evil, vile, base.

treachery N. treason, betrayal, disloyalty, perfidy.

tread V. step, walk, track.

treason N. betrayal, treachery, deception, subversion, sedition.

treasure N. prize, riches, gem, wealth, value.

treasury N. vault, bank, treasurehouse.

treat V. manage, handle, arrange; heal, attend; explain, interpret; host, indulge.

treatment N. regimen, therapy, care, attention.

treaty N. agreement, pact, alliance, charter, accord.

tremble V. vibrate, shake, pulsate, shudder, quiver.

• **tremendous** ADJ. enormous, giant, huge, amazing, marvelous. *An enormous cloud approached from the west.*

tremor N. earthquake, temblor, shudder, quiver, quake.

trespass V. intrude, encroach, invade, offend, breach.

trial N. test, examination, ordeal, crucible, hardship, difficulty.

tribute N. testimonial, compliment.

trick N. swindle, illusion, deception, fraud, artifice; —V. deceive, delude, cheat.

tricky ADJ. deceiving, delicate, tight, difficult, artful.

trim ADJ. compact, tidy, neat, clean, shapely.

trip N. journey, voyage, excursion; —V. stumble, slip, blunder.

trite ADJ. ordinary, dull, unimaginative, stupid, wearisome.

triumph N. achievement, defeat, conquest; —V. win, succeed, prevail, conquer.

triumphant ADJ. victorious, exultant, prevailing.

trivia N. minutiae, froth, triviality, trifles.

• **trivial** ADJ. unimportant, frivolous, insignificant, petty, small. *We have little time to debate unimportant details.*

troop N. company, assembly, party, group, army, soldiers; —V. assemble, throng.

trophy N. prize, award, plaque, token, memento.

trot V. lope, jog.

trouble N. distress, hardship, difficulty, inconvenience; —V. distress, disturb, worry, bother.

troublesome ADJ. disturbing, bothersome, annoying, upsetting, vexing.

truce N. ceasefire, peace, pause, armistice.

trudge V. shuffle, slog, drag, walk.

true ADJ. authentic, real, legitimate, genuine, factual, valid, correct.

trust N. faith, belief, confidence, certainty.

trustworthy ADJ. reliable, faithful, loyal, honest, reputable, dependable, authentic.

truth N. honesty, sincerity, fact, precision, veracity.

truthful ADJ. honest, frank, candid, veracious.

try V. test, use, tackle, experiment, undertake.

tug V. hold, draw, drag, tow, yank.

tumble V. roll, fall, trip, toss, stumble.

tumult N. disturbance, confusion, disorder, agitation, noise.

tune N. melody, harmony, air, song.

turbid ADJ. muddy, dense, thick, dark, opaque.

turbulent ADJ. tempestuous, stormy, tumultuous, rough.

turmoil N. uproar, pandemonium, disorder, unrest, agitation.

turn V. revolve, rotate, spin, sprain, deviate, avert; —N. bend, twist, shift, movement, circle.

twin ADJ. identical, double, similar, matched.

twinkle V. blink, flash, shine, sparkle.

twist V. distort, warp, bend, turn, wrinkle.

• **typical** ADJ. characteristic, classic, symbolic, usual, common. *A gruff manner is characteristic of the manager.*

tyrannize V. oppress, dictate, boss.

tyranny N. fascism, oppression, despotism, autocracy, dictatorship.

U

ugly ADJ. plain, unattractive, homely, rough, hideous.

ulterior ADJ. concealed, shrouded, obscured, covert, enigmatic, hidden.

ultimate ADJ. absolute, final, extreme, maximum, supreme.

unaccountable ADJ. mysterious, inexplicable, unexplained.

unadorned ADJ. rustic, plain, bare.

unadulterated ADJ. pure, original, natural.

unanimity N. consensus, accord, agreement.

unanimous ADJ. concurrent, in agreement, unified, solid.

unapproachable ADJ. intolerant, impossible, aloof.

unaware ADJ. uninformed, ignorant, blind.

unbearable ADJ. painful, distressing, agonizing.

unbecoming ADJ. improper, indecent, unfit, inappropriate.

unbelievable ADJ. implausible, fabulous, amazing, incredible.

unbending ADJ. rigid, firm, stubborn, determined, obstinate.

unblemished ADJ. good, clean, innocent, clear.

uncertain ADJ. doubtful, debatable, ambiguous, indefinite, irresolute.

uncivilized ADJ. crude, barbarous, savage, wild, primitive, rude.

unclear ADJ. indefinite, faint, vague, ambiguous, obscure.

uncomfortable ADJ. uneasy, awkward, harsh, distressing, comfortless.

unconditional ADJ. implicit, absolute, complete.

• **unconscious** ADJ. senseless, ignorant, cold. *After he fell, he lay senseless on the ground for more than an hour.*

uncover V. reveal, expose, unearth, betray.

undecided ADJ. indefinite, doubtful, ambiguous, unclear.

• **undeniable** ADJ. certain, sure, actual. *The facts in the case are certain.*

undependable ADJ. trustless, unreliable.

underground ADJ. subterranean, underneath; — N. resistance.

underhand ADJ. sneaky, devious, guileful, indirect.

underprivileged ADJ. poor, denied, depressed, suppressed.

• **understand** V. grasp, realize, conceive, know, comprehend. *The student found it difficult to grasp the unusual concept.*

understanding N. sympathy, empathy, knowledge, comprehension.

undertake V. try, attempt, assume, begin, start.

• **undesirable** ADJ. unwelcome, objectionable, unwanted. *Horseflies and other pests were unwelcome guests at the campsite.*

undo V. loosen, disengage, unbind, cancel.

undulate V. wave, rock, slither.

uneasy ADJ. nervous, anxious, edgy, restless.

unequivocal ADJ. sharp, definite, sure, utter.

unethical ADJ. wrong, corrupt, unscrupulous.

uneven ADJ. rough, unsteady, irregular, inconsistent.

unexplainable ADJ. mysterious, inexplicable.

unfair ADJ. unjust, wrong, unethical, biased, prejudiced, partial.

• **unfavorable** ADJ. disadvantageous, adverse, unsatisfactory, bad, negative. *The candidate excluded disadvantageous information from his résumé.*

unfit ADJ. inappropriate, unsuitable, improper, unqualified, unhealthy.

unforgivable ADJ. inexcusable, outrageous, extreme.

unfortunate ADJ. calamitous, unlucky, disastrous, untimely, ill-fated.

unhappy ADJ. sad, melancholy, miserable, depressed.

unify V. integrate, unite, organize, consolidate, connect.

uninspired ADJ. dull, laconic, apathetic, lethargic, lazy.

unintentional ADJ. unintended, inadvertent, unthinking, unplanned.

uninterested ADJ. detached, cold, distant, apathetic.

union N. association, confederation, league.

unique ADJ. unparalleled, matchless, only, original, single.

unite V. consolidate, combine, unify.

universal ADJ. total, comprehensive, cosmic, worldwide, global, general, broad.

universe N. cosmos, world, earth, heavens, galaxy.

unlawful ADJ. illegal, criminal, illicit, wrongful, lawless.

unlearned ADJ. ignorant, unscholarly, simple.

• **unlimited** ADJ. unrestricted, endless, limitless, boundless. *The bank offered unrestricted access to one's account.*

unload V. discharge, dump, remove.

unlucky ADJ. fateful, unfortunate, ill-fated, disappointing.

unmistakable ADJ. noticeable, observable.

unnatural ADJ. abnormal, bizarre, taboo, preternatural.

• **unnecessary** ADJ. needless, uncalled for, superfluous, pointless. *Some provisions of the contract were needless.*

unobtrusive ADJ. quiet, inconspicuous, subdued.

unpleasant ADJ. disagreeable, offensive, repulsive, bad.

unpretentious ADJ. informal, modest, humble.

unprincipled ADJ. unscrupulous, corrupt, immoral, lawless.

unprotected ADJ. insecure, helpless, open.

• **unreasonable** ADJ. outrageous, irrational, illogical. *The visitor's outrageous conduct led to his expulsion from the meeting.*

unreserved ADJ. open, free, unoccupied, implicit, plain.

unruly ADJ. disobedient, ungovernable, defiant, disorderly.

unsatisfactory ADJ. unfavorable, poor, bad.

unsettled ADJ. indefinite, restless, disturbed, anxious.

unsound ADJ. insane, mad, false, erroneous.

unsure ADJ. indefinite, ambiguous, insecure.

unsympathetic ADJ. removed, cold, untouched, uncaring.

unusual ADJ. abnormal, extraordinary, infrequent, atypical, eccentric, novel.

unwelcome ADJ. unwanted, undesirable, objectionable, uninvited.

unwholesome ADJ. dangerous, unhealthy, demoralizing, offensive, corrupting.

unyielding ADJ. rigid, stubborn, severe, inflexible.

upgrade V. promote, improve, better.

uplift V. elevate, inspire, exalt, elate.

uproar N. disturbance, commotion, noise, disorder.

upset V. topple, overturn, disorder, agitate, disrupt; disturb, bother, pain; —N. agitation, disruption, disordering.

urge V. push, press, insist, implore, persuade, recommend.

use V. implement, utilize, employ, apply; consume, expend, abuse.

- **usually** ADV. typically, consistently, generally, normally, regularly, frequently, commonly. *Bulbs are typically planted in the early fall.*

usurp V. seize, appropriate, assume, take, claim.

utter ADJ. complete, extreme, absolute, entire, sheer; —V. speak, announce, declare, assert, talk.

V

vacant ADJ. empty, unoccupied, uninhabited, vapid, thoughtless.

vacation N. break, holiday, respite, rest.

vacillate V. change, sway, hesitate, alter, fluctuate.

• **vague** ADJ. indefinite, unclear, ambiguous, uncertain, obscure. *I could make out only the indefinite outline of the large building in the distance.*

vain ADJ. trivial, frivolous, narcissistic, proud, conceited, egotistic, futile, empty.

valid ADJ. authentic, real, sound, genuine.

valor N. heroism, courage, bravery.

• **valuable** ADJ. expensive, costly, treasured, prized, priceless. *Expensive jewelry should be kept in the hotel safe.*

value N. price, worth, importance, usefulness, utility; —V. appraise, treasure, revere.

vanish V. disappear, fade, evaporate, dissolve.

variation N. fluctuation, deviation, change, variance, diversity.

• **variety** N. mixture, difference, diversity, assortment, heterogeneity. *The pet's ancestry included a mixture of breeds.*

various ADJ. diverse, mixed, assorted, varied, miscellaneous.

vary V. alter, change, differ.

vein N. streak, mood, style.

vend V. sell, peddle, market.

vent N. hole, opening; —V. emit, air, discharge, release, expel.

venture N. peril, risk, hazard, attempt, experiment.

veracity N. truthfulness, truth, reality, sincerity, fidelity, honest.

verbal ADJ. oral, spoken, literal, lingual, vocal.

verbatim ADJ. literal, word-for-word.

verge N. point, brink, edge, border, margin.

verify V. affirm, corroborate, prove, confirm.

versatile ADJ. multifaceted, adaptable, skillful, flexible, ready.

very ADV. greatly, extremely, exceedingly, thoroughly, highly.

veteran N. old-timer, campaigner; —ADJ. practical, experienced.

veto V. refuse, deny, negate, reject, prohibit.

vicious ADJ. fierce, evil, cruel, malevolent.

victim N. scapegoat, puppet, prey, sacrifice.

victor N. winner, champion, conqueror.

view N. perspective, outlook, belief, sight, scene.

vigil N. wake, lookout, watch, observance.

vigilant ADJ. alert, attentive, watchful, observant.

vigor N. vitality, energy, drive, spirit, strength.

vindicate V. avenge, defend, clear, assert.

vindictive ADJ. vengeful, spiteful, malicious, relentless.

vintage N. classic, year; —ADJ. classical.

violent ADJ. intense, forceable, strong, savage, rough.

virtue N. merit, distinction, excellence, good, chastity.

virulent ADJ. malignant, deadly, poisonous, baneful, resentful.

visible ADJ. perceptible, apparent, visual.

vision N. dream, foresight, prophecy, sight, seeing.

visit V. attend, call on, see, drop in.

vital ADJ. critical, essential, necessary, important, alive, existing.

vivacious ADJ. exuberant, animated, spirited, lively.

vocabulary N. language, lexicon, dictionary.

vocal ADJ. oral, spoken, uttered, articulate, voiced.

vociferous ADJ. loud, clamorous, vehement, blatant, unruly.

voice N. intonation, speech, expression; —V. declare, express, utter, speak.

void ADJ. unoccupied, hollow, empty, destitute.

voluntary ADJ. deliberate, intentional, spontaneous.

vulgar ADJ. lowly, rude, coarse, ignorant, uncouth.

W

wage V. pursue, conduct, engage in, carry out.

wager N., V. bet, gamble, stake, risk.

wail V. scream, howl, bawl, cry.

wait V. linger, remain, pause, delay, serve, attend.

waive V. defer, abdicate, relinquish.

wake V. arouse, stir, waken; —N. vigil.

wakeful ADJ. awake, alert, sleepless, unsleeping.

walk V. stroll, promenade, amble, hike, step.

wall N. partition, barrier, bar.

wander V. roam, stroll, drift, stray, meander.

want V. desire, need, lack; —N. insufficiency, desire, necessity, need.

wanton ADJ. gratuitous, unnecessary, easy, immoral.

warfare N. combat, battle, conflict, fighting, struggle.

warm ADJ. sympathetic, compassionate, approachable, kind, tepid, feverish.

warn V. admonish, caution, alert, appraise.

warp V. bend, twist, distort.

warrant V. guarantee, pledge; —N. assurance, license.

wary ADJ. careful, cautious, prudent, alert.

wash V. clean, scrub, drift, bathe.

waste N. trash, garbage, loss, consumption; —V. consume, squander, abuse, exhaust, devastate.

wasteful ADJ. extravagant, lavish, careless, reckless, destructive, prodigal.

watch V. observe, look, scrutinize.

watchful ADJ. prudent, careful, wary, alert, cautious.

water V. irrigate, wet, soak, wash.

watery ADJ. diluted, pale, insipid.

way N. system, method, fashion, mode, behavior; avenue, path, street, road.

• **weak** ADJ. feeble, helpless, exhausted, languid, faint. *The flu left the patient exhausted and feeble.*

weaken V. exhaust, reduce, impair, debilitate, diminish, dilute.

weakness N. infirmity, fault, failing, shortcoming.

wealth N. riches, money, opulence, means, prosperity.

wear V. carry, use, dress in, attire, bear, diminish, erode, waste.

weary ADJ. tired, exhausted, discouraged, bored.

weave V. braid, twist, crochet, intertwine, knit.

web N. net, network, mesh.

wed V. marry, espouse.

weep V. cry, lament, sob.

weigh V. ponder, consider, steady.

weight N. mass, heaviness, authority, significance, importance.

weighty ADJ. burdensome, heavy, significant, important.

- **weird** ADJ. strange, odd, bizarre, eerie, peculiar.
  They observed a strange array of moving lights in the midnight sky.

welfare N. good, prosperity, fortune, advantage.

well ADV. satisfactorily, completely, favorably, considerably; healthy, certainly, surely.

wet ADJ. drenched, soaked, damp, moist, saturated.

wheel N. disk, circle, roller, revolution.

whimsical ADJ. capricious, fanciful, wondrous, arbitrary.

whine V. cry, whimper, complain.

whip V. beat, lash, defeat.

whirl V. spin, rush, swirl.

whisper V. murmur, confide, mutter.

whole ADJ. entire, complete, total, undivided, absolute.

wholesome ADJ. nourishing, healthy, clean, good.

wholly ADV. completely, purely, entirely, totally.

wicked ADJ. evil, vicious, wrong, vile, malevolent.

wide ADJ. broad, full, extensive.

widen V. extend, broaden, stretch.

width N. wideness, breadth, broadness.

wiggle V. twist, squirm, worm, writhe.

wild ADJ., ADV. natural, untamed, native, savage, rough, frantic, unruly.

will N. desire, wish, determination, decision, resolve.

willful ADJ. deliberate, strong, stubborn, obstinate.

wilt V. slouch, droop, sag.

win V. earn, succeed, obtain, attain, capture, gain.

wind N. gust, draft, breeze, air; —V. curl, weave, twist, coil.

winding ADJ. meandering, twisting, curving.

windy ADJ. breezy, blustering, stormy.

winner N. conqueror, victor, champion.

wipe out V. cancel, annihilate, eliminate.

wisdom N. insight, intelligence, acumen, commonsense, sagacity, good sense.

wise ADJ. shrewd, insightful, rational, enlightened, sensible, profound, sage.

wish V. desire, choose, crave, want.

wit N. humor, intelligence, understanding, wisdom.

witch N. magician, sorceress, warlock, enchanter.

withdraw V. retract, detach, recall, remove.

wither V. dry up, shrivel, fade, languish.

withhold V. repress, hold back, refuse, refrain.

witness N. attester, observer, spectator; —V. observe, perceive, notice, see.

witty ADJ. clever, humorous, funny.

wobbly ADJ. insecure, hesitant, unstable.

woe N. distress, grief, sorrow.

womanly ADJ. feminine, effeminate.

wonder N. awe, admiration, marvel, amazement, dread.

word N. remark, comment, vocable, statement, assurance, term, guarantee, expression.

wording N. phrase, wordage, diction.

wordy ADJ. long-winded, verbose, talkative, garrulous.

work N. labor, effort, employment, job; —V. perform, operate, run.

worldly ADJ. materialistic, earthly, profane, secular.

worn ADJ. tired, exhausted, weary, used, threadbare.

worry V. annoy, irritate, disturb, fret, trouble; — N. anxiety, doubt, concern.

worth N. value, merit, estimation, importance, price.

● **worthless** ADJ. inferior, useless, valueless, insignificant, unimportant. *The inspector rejected the inferior products.*

worthy ADJ. reliable, dependable, good, honorable, valuable.

wrap V. clothe, envelop, shroud, veil, package.

wrath N. fury, anger, rage.

wreck V. destroy, damage, ruin, trash.

wrench V. jerk, twist, ring, distort, turn.

wrinkle N., V., fold, crease, crumple, crimp.

write V. compose, record, inscribe, draft.

writhe V. squirm, wiggle, agonize, toss, twist.

wrong ADJ. false, erroneous, evil; —N. sin, cruelty, malevolence.

wrongdoing N. crime, misbehavior, injury, sin.

wrongful ADJ. criminal, unlawful, evil, spiteful, illegal.

X Y Z

x out V. cancel, omit, cross out, erase.

yank V. jerk, pull, tug.

yarn N. fable, tale, story, anecdote, legend.

yawn V. nap, doze, snooze.

yearn V. wish for, desire, crave.

yeast N. catalyst, foam.

yell V. shout, cry, roar, scream, howl.

yes ADV. agreed, absolutely, certainly, gladly, willingly, OK.

yet ADV. still, however, furthermore, although; — CONJ. but, nevertheless.

yield V. defer, relinquish, succumb, return, surrender, abdicate.

• **young** ADJ. juvenile, immature, infantile, new. *The theater offered special prices for juvenile customers.*

youth N. immaturity, adolescence, springtime, youthfulness.

zany ADJ. foolish, amusing, wacky, comical, madcap.

zeal N. enthusiasm, fervor, passion, involvement, eagerness.

zephyr N. breeze, wind, air, draft.

zero N. nothing, naught, nobody, void, nil, nonentity.

zest N. desire, pleasure, relish, enjoyment, exhilaration, enthusiasm, gusto, vigor.